# CAREERS
## IN COMMUNICATIONS

## SHONAN F. R. NORONHA

**VGM Career Horizons**
a division of *NTC Publishing Group*
Lincolnwood, Illinois USA

**Library of Congress Cataloging-in-Publication Data**

Noronha, Shonan F. R.
    Careers in communications / Shonan Noronha.
        p.    cm. — (VGM professional careers series)
    ISBN 0-8442-4182-2. — ISBN 0-8442-4183-0 (pbk.)
    1. Communication—Vocational guidance—United States.  2. Mass
media—Vocational guidance—United States.  I. Title.  II. Series.
P91.6.N67   1993
384′.023′73—dc20                                                   93-25152
                                                                    CIP

Published by VGM Career Horizons, a division of NTC Publishing Group
4255 West Touhy Avenue
Lincolnwood (Chicago), Illinois 60646-1975, U.S.A.

3 4 5 6 7 8 9 0 VP 9 8 7 6 5 4 3 2 1

# ABOUT THE AUTHOR

Writer, producer, educator, and internationally recognized authority on mass media communications, Shonan F. R. Noronha is president of Media Resources, a New York-based consulting firm serving the media, corporations, and educational institutions. Her essays and articles on television and education have been published in journals and industry magazines all over the world.

Noronha was awarded a Doctor of Education degree in Educational Technology by Teachers College, Columbia University in 1979. She also earned Master of Education and Master of Arts degrees from Columbia University. She completed her media studies from the Xavier Institute of Communication Arts, Bombay, after receiving a Bachelor of Arts degree from the University of Bombay, India.

Dr. Noronha was founder and editor-in-chief of several trade publications, among them *Tour & Travel News: The Newspaper for the Leisure Travel Industry* for CMP Publications; and *International Television: The Journal of the International Television Association* (ITVA) for Ziff-Davis Publishing Company. Prior to joining Ziff-Davis, she was technical director of EPIE (Educational Products Information Exchange) Institute.

Noronha's broadcast experience spans two decades and includes production work with PBS (Public Broadcasting System), New York; Radio Telefis Eireann, Ireland; and All India Radio & Television. She was also TV host of the International Youth Program during the early days of New York's cable television.

Dr. Noronha was assistant professor at Iona College, New Rochelle, New York. She was also adjunct associate professor at the Graduate School of Corporate and Political Communications, Fairfield University, Connecticut. She is frequently invited by corporations and universities to lecture on the applications of new communications technologies, and her research work is the basis of design decisions made by several communications hardware and software companies.

Dr. Shonan Noronha has written and produced training and marketing programs, in a variety of media, for a broad spectrum of corporate and institutional clients. She has also served on judging panels of domestic and international video festivals.

# ACKNOWLEDGMENTS

The expertise of a number of people has made this book possible. To all of them, my deep and sincere gratitude. Some of my colleagues, friends, and family members deserve special recognition for their individual contribution to *Careers in Communications.*

To Fred Schmidt, a very special thank you. I had the privilege of working with him when he was editorial director of *Photomethods, International Television,* and *Photo Design*. Credit for the chapter on photography belongs to him.

A major contribution was made by Dr. George Thottam, Department of Communications, Iona College, New York. He shares his breadth of knowledge in the field of journalism in Chapter 2.

Career information for the audiovisual specialist came from Billy Bowles, director of VisNet, GTE Service Corporation. Brian Boucher, a communications consultant in New York provided current information on multimedia.

John Rhodes, an expert in the applications of new media technologies, shares his insights on Emerging Technologies and the changing job market in each area of the communications industry.

I am grateful to Harry McGee, executive vice president, International Communications Industries Association (ICIA) for writing the foreword.

Beyond these principal contributors, I am deeply indebted to my sister Sirikit Noronha for being the motivating force that saw this project to fruition. She administered large doses of humor and chocolate when adrenalin was low.

The staff of several organizations assisted me in compiling the reference material which is an essential part of *Careers in Communications.* I am grateful, in particular, to the library and publications editorial staff of Public Relations Society of America (PRSA), Audio Engineering Society (AES), and National Association of Broadcasters (NAB).

Finally, my thanks to my past, present, and future students for providing the best reason to write this book.

Shonan F. R. Noronha
New York, NY

# FOREWORD

Goods jobs—like good books—are hard to find.

For those seeking careers in communications today, the task is daunting indeed. The best approach to finding the niche that's right for you is an organized one, as Shonan Noronha clearly points out in *Careers in Communications.*

While effective communicators are the lifeblood of business, industry, government, and education, often the most difficult aspect of working in this field is landing a job.

Dr. Noronha shows great good sense in her research and explanation of career opportunities in this exciting and rewarding field. She examines the most important areas of communications today—journalism, photography, radio, television, film, multimedia, public relations, and advertising.

The author gives readers concrete advice on where the jobs are and how to get them. In addition to practical guidance, *Careers in Communications* provides valuable job search resources, including appendices on trade associations, publications, and directories.

As a communications professional, Dr. Noronha is well aware that the skills involved in every people-to-people act—to educate, to train, to motivate—are at once a science and an art. Yet she manages to present an overview of this complex field which is easy to read and understand.

Dr. Noronha succinctly and fairly states the case for present day opportunities in communications. Her well-written book is for those who wish to acquire the skills—and practice the art—of effective communication.

Harry R. McGee, CAE
Executive Vice President
International Communications Industries Association

# PREFACE

Communications is a multi-faceted industry offering exciting and challenging career opportunities. *Careers in Communications* is designed to give you a comprehensive picture of each of these facets. It reaches into the various fields of practice encompassed by this dynamic industry—an industry in which trillions of dollars are spent on the creation and distribution of words, sounds, and images. The broad spectrum of all communications activity has this at its focal point: the core and purpose of the message.

*Careers in Communications* details the fundamental skills necessary for the design, production, and distribution of a message—be it to inform, to teach, to persuade, or to entertain. There is a chapter on each media profession—journalism, photography, film, radio/audio, audiovisual/multimedia, television/video, advertising, and public relations. Each chapter is self-contained. Each contains information on the nature of jobs, where the jobs are, and the skills and training required for specific jobs. You will also find listings of directories and other sources useful in your job search efforts.

While your initial interest in using this book may be solely with the section devoted to the medium of your interest, you may also want to explore the information in the chapters on other communications media. Because most jobs in the communications industry are interrelated, having a comprehensive view of the job possibilities will enhance your understanding of whatever career path you choose, and how it relates to the rest of the industry.

The lure of mass media communications has often been its technology. The technological developments of each medium from instant photography to laser recording of sound and video continue to accelerate at a dizzying pace. This has led to increased and varied job opportunities.

The kaleidoscopic manner in which technical advances are being made adds to the fascination of working in this industry.

The objective of this book is to present the information basic to a comprehensive and pragmatic approach to working in a continually evolving industry. Toward that end, this book will help you determine the area in which your talents and skills may best be utilized. As a resource in itself and a guide to other resources, *Careers in Communications* provides you with the information necessary to get started in the media and to move on to achieving full professional productivity in the medium of your choice and the communications industry at large.

## EMERGING TECHNOLOGIES AND THE COMMUNICATIONS JOB MARKET

Emerging technologies have continued to change the nature of the communications professions at an ever more rapid pace in the 1990s. Aspiring communicators would do well to aggressively acquire skills with the appropriate technological tools mentioned in the following paragraphs.

**Journalism:** All areas of journalism have eagerly adopted technologies that enable reporters and editors to do a better and faster job. Laptop computers with high-speed modems—linked to desktop publishing systems—linked to automated service bureaus and printing plants have all but taken the paper out of print journalism.

The growing tendency to compile and distribute newsworthy information on-line and via CD-ROM presage an even greater revolution in this area. The use of electronic photo journalism, portable satellite uplinks, and desktop video and multimedia editing systems are but a few of the technologies that will even further accelerate the evolution of journalism.

**Photography:** Electronic photography is revolutionizing the nature of a field that had previously seen slow steady changes over the past fifty years. The ability to shoot, process, transmit, and edit images instantly has obvious attraction for photo journalists and industrial photographers. CCD chips of ever-increasing quality and decreasing cost have opened the electronic floodgate. Adobe Photoshop and similar programs have amplified the imagination of pre-press designers. JPEG compression, CD-ROM storage and publishing of photographs (e.g., Kodak Photo CD), visual database and cataloging systems (e.g., Aldus Fetch), color copiers, and video "printers" have just begun to change, forever, the way we store, retrieve, and publish images.

The deployment of EP (electronic photography) has also been accelerated in some application areas because of environmental concerns. Many organizations find themselves facing mandates to severely restrict water use, and EP is a natural solution to this dilemma.

**Video Production/Post-Production:** Digital video, Desktop video, CCD cameras, studio automation, component cassette formats— video production and post-production have benefited tremendously from the growth of these new technologies, and others, over the past few years.

The good news is that new creative capabilities and plummeting hardware costs have created a boom in professional video, which is meeting the demand created by the expanding cable and home video markets.

The bad news is that a sluggish economy, corporate consolidations, and the spread of pro-sumer video have put a two-sided squeeze on the video job market. Doing more with less is the order of the day—from broadcast studios where the talent may be the only thing that breathes, to local news channels covering a metropolis with a few dozen producer-reporter-editor-programming-type people.

The brightest side of this high-tech "downsizing" mode is the opportunity for modest startups to hit the big time (or at least look like it). Small independent producers working with devices like the "Video Toaster" have landed major production sub-contracts, based on creative ability instead of a big budget.

There are still plenty of great opportunities in production and post production, but top-notch technical, artistic, and people skills are a baseline for getting out of a tape library job these days.

**Film:** The most significant changes in the area of film have not been in film technology itself but in the application of new video technologies to film.

The use of HDTV (high-definition television) and computer graphics for feature film special effects, as in "The Empire Strikes Back", "The Last Starfighter", and many others, has expanded creative horizons and further blurred the (mostly business and traditional) barriers separating video, film, graphics, and other visual disciplines. Off-line dailies (pioneered by Coppola), and the growing trend to "get it in the can" in HDTV (especially for music video), irrespective of current release format, have made it even more important for those planning careers in the film industry to have more than a passing familiarity with the advantages (and limitations) of these new technologies.

**Public Relations:** The public relations industry, being deeply involved in public perception, has been in the forefront in its employment of new media. This deployment has been in direct proportion to the ability of those new media to "get the word out," and to affect the perception of the targeted audience. Distribution of press releases and other information via E-Mail, electronic bulletin boards (BBSs), and public information utilities (CompuServe, Delphi, etc.), fax, computer disc, and even CD-ROM is an increasingly common practice. The gathering of information via these same channels is also becoming a routine matter. PR agencies and corporate communications departments have used business television (via satellite) for years to get their message out, and video "press releases" have reportedly provided a cheap source of news footage to many TV stations. More recently, the use of interactive Videoconferencing for interviews and press conferences has enabled key executives to be in "two places at once." The bottom line for the future of an aspiring public relations professional is an open mind to the abilities of new communications technologies to influence public perceptions.

**Advertising:** The advertising industry has kept pace with the development of new media, and in many cases it has been a driving force in the widespread use of these. Future "Ad-Persons" will need to be comfortable with a full spectrum of media for research, production, and delivery of their clients' messages.

While ad agencies have been aggressive in the use of Infomercials, Narrowcasting, and interactive media (such as videotext and other multimedia) for public consumption, they have been equally advanced in the internal use of such tools as desktop graphics/publishing, on-line demographic databases, bio-feedback monitoring of test audiences, and multimedia training and communications.

The use of interactive media for advertising purposes is increasing at a steady pace. Offering easily quantifiable results, access to sharply defined populations, and quite a bit of "sizzle" for the buck, such media as Prodigy (an on-line videotext-based utility), and videodisc-based kiosks in malls and airports are gaining in popularity. "Home shopping" channels, which offer a crude form of interactive participation, are growing rapidly, with major retailers jumping on the bandwagon as we go to press.

In the future, "T.V. On-Demand" will not only offer viewers the choice of hundreds of branching channels but will also provide advertisers the capacity for truly interactive "live" video catalog shopping.

**Multimedia:** Multimedia is a catch-all designation for all the new communications technologies that don't fit into the old categories. Ten years ago multimedia referred to interactive videodisc-based training and information systems, and was sometimes used to designate shows combining various media such as slides, video, film, audio-tape, and other elements.

Multimedia today encompasses not only the various optical disc-based systems but all production, delivery, and presentation systems using microcomputers to combine print, graphics, sound, and possibly animation and motion video—whether the element of interactivity is present or not.

It is feasible today for a single talented multimedia specialist to produce in a few days, with a $5,000 Macintosh system, an educational or commercial presentation that would have occupied an entire team, with hundreds of thousands of dollars of equipment, just a few years ago. This same presentation can be delivered to a distant user's desktop in seconds via switched digital lines and high speed LANs, as compared to the weeks previously required to publish and distribute the "old-fashioned" optical media. This is not to say that production companies and CD-

ROM are obsolete, but rather to suggest that the cost/time/impact for-mula for multimedia continues to evolve at an ever more rapid pace.

With multimedia entering the mass market through SEGA, Nintendo, IBM, Apple, and others, the opportunities for those with the skills and imagination to master these difficult tools are virtually limitless.

# CONTENTS

# DEDICATION

This book is dedicated to my mother and father, who nurtured achievement. Their tremendous enthusiasm for every task I take on and pride in even my smallest accomplishments propels me toward new goals.

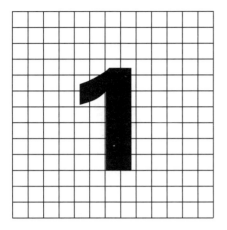

# INTRODUCTION

The communications technology revolution continues to radically change our private and professional lives. It is doing so not only by its speed of development but also by the way in which it affects our economic, social, and political systems. With the ability of computers and satellites instantly to link several cities in the world, we have seen the birth of global electronic banking, an expansion of international trade, and, most dramatic of all, "live" television coverage of news events, as they happen, almost anywhere in the world.

Today's sophisticated communications systems are delivering information faster and to more locations than ever before. The integration of computer, telephone, and satellite technologies is responsible for this faster flow of information that has led society into the Information Age. We now mass-produce and almost instantly disseminate information that, in turn, accelerates the pace of commerce. The business world pants for information—up-to-date data on which to make decisions; "how-to" information, delivering the most innovative techniques to problem-solving; and not least, "opportunity" information presenting a smorgasbord of growth and success venues.

All sectors of society are demanding more information. This tremendous need for a continuous flow of information is creating many new career opportunities for information specialists trained in the various communications media. The proliferation of information has resulted in a dire need for communications specialists who can sort and select information, as well as create new information and tailor-make messages for specific audiences. The continuously changing environment in which we live imposes new pressures on the relationships between individuals, groups, and organizations. This increases the need for organizations to communicate effectively with individuals, thereby increasing the demand for skilled communicators. Professional communicators play a critical role in our society's shift to an information-based economy.

## WHAT PROFESSIONAL COMMUNICATORS DO

Communications is the process of transmitting ideas, information, and attitudes from person to person. Mass communications is organized communications, directed to a large number of people for a specific purpose, via established mass media channels. Professional communicators are those who are in the business of designing, producing, and distributing information to specific audiences.

Words, sounds, and images are the means by which communicators convey messages to their audiences. Hence, professional communicators must be adept at the techniques of word, sound, and image recording, creation, and manipulation to design effective messages. All organized communications serve one or more of the four basic functions: to inform, to educate, to persuade, and to entertain.

Traditional mass media—namely books, magazines, newspapers, films, radio, and television—are designed to meet various communications functions. The electronic media, broadcast television in particular, offers communicators a vehicle through which they can present an idea to motivate, inform, persuade, and inspire audiences. Communications professionals have the responsibility of establishing and maintaining effective relationships with their audiences. Those who are adept in communication arts can persuade their audiences to take desired courses of action or make certain decisions.

Communications professions include journalism, photography, audiovisual and multimedia, radio and television broadcasting, film, advertising, and public relations. Each of these media use special techniques and technologies for the creation and display or distribution of a message. Each medium calls into play the specialized skills of trained people in the field. Hence, communicators today should have the underpinnings of communications theory as well as the necessary skills to utilize communications technology.

The communications industry is all pervasive. In addition to media companies, career opportunities for professional communicators exist in all types of organizations—business and industry, government and military, education institutions, medicine, and nonprofit institutions. The area of business or organizational communications is rapidly expanding. Organizational communicators need to draw from the same collage of skills as do media communicators. They need to communicate with internal audiences, such as employees, as well as external audiences, such as customers, shareholders, and the local community. In a highly competitive environment, an organization's need to communicate with its varied audiences increases. Consequently, there is an increased need for trained and experienced communicators.

## DEVELOPMENTS IN COMMUNICATIONS TECHNOLOGY

Advancements in computer, video, and satellite technologies are changing the ways in which we meet today's communications needs. *Electronic publishing systems* are reducing the time and cost of publishing a wide range of material. The variety of products incorporated into such systems include micro- and mainframe computers, phototypesetting equipment, laser printers, and software that integrates these elements. The most elaborate and expensive systems are being used for text-intensive and high-volume production of newspapers, magazines, and catalogs. Less expensive, personal computer-based systems that allow the user to compose text with graphics into pages are increasingly being used by corporations to produce office reports and company newsletters.

*Computer Graphics* is one of the fastest growing segments of the visual communications industry. It has enhanced the presentation quality of business information tremendously. Today's computerized imaging devices are a great boon: they allow us to create, manipulate, store, and retrieve images with artistic flair, flexibility, and speed. Digital effects, paint, and animation systems offer producers astounding effects to give impact to their message. Image creation: you can select a color palette from literally 16 million colors. Some systems allow you to select a pattern or texture and then insert it into a specified area. Color mixing is a universal feature of these systems, as is freehand sketching and painting. Image manipulation: once limited to switchers, manipulation is now performed on specialized units. Wipes, mattes, simple animation, and the relocation of still pictures across the screen—all this is now within the grasp of even low-budget producers. Those with more money talk posterizations and strobe effects. The high-end units can rotate entire images at right angles to the audience, explore three-dimensional space, and animate still pictures in real time. Millions and millions of dollars are being spent on computerized images today—some on business, most on commercials and the entertainment media.

*Television production equipment* has developed rapidly, putting new and improved tools in the hands of the producer—everything from affordable CCD cameras to user-friendly editing systems to high-definition television (HDTV) products. The miniaturization of video cameras and recorders has taken video and television into remote corners of the world: all this to document events; educate people; motivate them to buy products and services, or concepts and ideas; and entertain them at home.

Developments in satellite technologies have made it possible to target messages to specific viewers through the mass media. The emergence and growth of cable television stations has led to specialized programming such as all-news services and all-sports stations. The development of Direct Broadcast Satellites is making a significant contribution toward the free flow of information across national boundaries. For the business communicator, advances in satellite technology have led to the greater use of teleconferences.

No longer is creativity in film and television production constrained by the limitations of the equipment. Today, it can only be limited by the imagination of the artist or communicator.

What all this means to a person considering a career as a professional communicator is that the tools of the trade to make any message and reach any audience already exist. You must learn how to use them, as well as understand the scope and limitations of each. Much too often, students of communications, in an attempt to master the technology, overlook the more important challenge of understanding the process. It is our task as professional communicators to know the full range of technology available and the capability of each to improve the quality of our messages. As visual communicators, we should also bear in mind a communication guru's advice: "If a picture is worth a thousand words, be sure that the words make sense, and the image says what you mean."

## TECHNOLOGY: CHANGING THE NATURE OF JOBS

While providing professional communicators with powerful tools, new technologies are also putting greater demands on them. They are changing the very nature of several media jobs. Sophisticated equipment enables communicators to work with speed and ease; it also imposes a different standard of performance. The concepts of *deadline* and *quality* take on new meanings.

The race for fast-breaking new stories has put enormous pressure on wire services and newspapers. Computerized typesetting and quick-printing presses have pushed newspaper deadlines close to early hours of the day for morning papers. That, in turn, has made the work of reporters and editors more demanding, both in terms of the number of hours they spend on the job and the pressure to get "up-to-the-minute" information. Computers and video display terminals on reporters' desks are adding to the tasks of reporters. They are now expected to do a lot more editing and layout work on their stories.

The move toward electronic publishing made by many publishers is leading to the elimination of some jobs in typesetting and printing. Some newspapers now have the capability of computerized full pagination that allows editors to prepare the whole page, ready for platemaking and printing. Thus, many functions today, including the tasks of the layout artist, can be handled by editors or other workers.

Modern technology is demanding more mechanical and technological skills from today's communicator. In the past, familiarity with the keyboard of a typewritter could earn a living for a print journalist. Today, skill in word processing and computer graphics are increasingly required, as well as familiarity with distribution technologies such as videotext, teletext, viewdata, and facsimile transmission.

Microwave technology applied to ENG (Electronic News Gathering) has revolutionized the broadcast newsroom. Today, a television journalist can carry a portable camera and portable microwave transmitter into the scene of action and proceed to conduct "live" interviews. A nearby mobile van equipped with a microwave transmitter and antenna receives the signal and transmits it back to the television station. The miniaturization of technology and the facility for satellite transmission has made it possible to telecast an event as it happens from almost anywhere in the world. Along with this technology comes the pressure for disseminating news without any delay. Radio and television newscasters and reporters have to be quicker thinkers, writers, and speakers today than ever before.

New roles and uses of the media are being explored, and with them come new jobs and career options. People who are imaginative, flexible, and aggressive seek such options and succeed in communications. As professional communicators, we should strive to go beyond the satisfaction of getting our jobs done well; we ought to think of what we can do with the media to enlighten people.

## FANTASY AND REALITY

One of the biggest illusions of contemporary society is the glamor of mass media professions. The power of the media and the apparent grandeur and mystique of the technology involved may be responsible for these illusions. In addition, the idealism attached, for example, to journalism as a media profession makes it one of the most popular career choices of young people even before they finish high school.

While many careers, such as medicine, law, engineering, and architecture, demand high intellectual abilities, many people seem to believe that a career in communications does not. Almost everybody feels competent to be a critic, reporter, anchorperson, or film director. This simplistic notion of the demands of the communication professions seems to attract a lot of indecisive minds to the world of communications. Their goal is the movie set of Hollywood; the office of *The Washington Post* as featured in *All the President's Men;* the anchor desk of ABC's Ted Koppel; or the exciting on-the-air personality of a favorite DJ. The reality, more often than not, is far from such fantasies.

The communications industry is fast-paced and exciting, as well as challenging and demanding. A career in this industry calls for a well-rounded education and a strong sense of commitment. Communications as a profession can bring you job satisfaction as well as financial rewards. You must, however, invest some time in proper career planning. The chapters that follow provide a picture of each of the fields of communications practice and will help you determine your precise area of interest for work as a professional communicator. Beyond that, this book serves as a practical guide to seeking a position in the business.

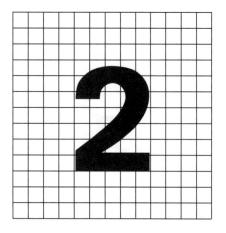

# JOURNALISM

Editors, hiring new reporters seek dedication and talent, but also demand college training, with a preference for journalism degrees.*

---

*Reporting Processes and Practices: News Writing for Today's Readers. Everette E. Dennis and Arnold H. Ismach. Wadsworth Publishing Co., Belmont, CA.

The world of journalism is much wider than that of a few national newspapers and scores of tabloids. American journalism has come a long way since colonial days when newspapers served as organs of commercial and political information. Today, the term *journalism* is applied to throwaway shoppers found at supermarket doors, to prestigious publications such as *The New York Times,* and to television news operations such as *60 Minutes* and *NBC Nightly News.*

First Amendment rights and the democratic political environment of the United States have contributed to the uninhibited growth of the news media in public and private communication. The United States can pride itself on supporting the largest mass media system of any country in the world, thanks to free enterprise in most media. The media in turn have generated millions of jobs and become major industrial forces that support the nation's economy.

The "fourth estate" today includes not only newspapers but also wire services and syndicates, radio and television, and trade and business publications, yet the role of journalism remains the same: to report and interpret information to the general public or some specific subgroup. However, the nature of the industry has changed considerably, due to socioeconomic changes and technological innovations.

The invention of new technologies has changed the nature of the journalism industry, making it an increasingly sophisticated and complex operation that requires a wide range of skills. Journalism has come a long way since the days of commercial printers who single-handedly published newsbooks and newsletters, and of radio stations that were one-person operations from private homes. Even many small town newspapers and radio stations today employ advanced production technology and the services of professionally trained journalists and skilled production people.

The demands of contemporary society have expanded the role of journalism. Newspapers and broadcast stations provide a great variety of services today. Besides reporting and interpreting news, they also entertain their audience with a variety of feature material. Newspapers, magazines, and broadcast stations are constantly competing with each other to capture the audience as it is crucial to their advertising revenues and sales.

The socioeconomic structure of the United States today has added new functions for journalists. Organizational demands have created thousands of company and organizational publications that are something more than mimeographed newsletters. Publications for internal and external communications has become an integral part of most organizations today.

The evolution of journalism into a massive industry has resulted in a number of related jobs in production, circulation, advertising, publicity, promotion, and management. Newspapers and broadcast stations employ specialists in all of these areas. The number of allied jobs in news organizations has substantially increased in recent years, and many job seekers are unaware of these career opportunities.

Still, aspiring journalists dream of being like Woodward, Bernstein, Cronkite, or Walters. Harsh realities of a highly competitive market and the stresses and strains of an extremely demanding profession stand between them and greatness. While traditionally well-defined jobs are decreasing in American journalism due to the decline of major daily newspapers, new avenues are being opened every day by advancing technology and the everchanging needs of society. For those who are innovative, creative, and aggressive, there is still a place in the exciting world of journalism.

### THE JOBS

To many recent graduates of journalism schools or departments, a job in journalism means *reporting* or even *investigative reporting*. Unfortunately, not even one fourth of the staff members of a newspaper are reporters. The market is very competitive, and entry level jobs at newspapers are hard to get. Enterprising candidates look beyond newspapers for a career in journalism. Wire services, syndicates, magazines, and radio and television stations offer reporting, writing, editing, and other related jobs.

**Newspapers**

Daily newspapers (1,710) and weekly newspapers (7,500) constitute the third largest industry in the United States, employing 450,000 people. Most of the dailies are evening newspapers. The number of major metropolitan dailies has declined in recent years; only 35 papers have a circulation of over 250,000 copies. On the other hand, group ownership has grown; about 65 percent of the newspapers are owned by groups.

Large and medium-sized newspapers have the following departments: news, editorial, advertising, production, circulation, and business. In smaller papers, these functions are often combined; the same person may handle several of these responsibilities.

Jobs in the news department include those of *reporter, rewrite, feature writer, columnist, critic,* and *photographer*. Entry-level jobs of *researcher* and *messenger* are also available in large dailies. The editorial department consists of *city editors* and *section editors* who are responsible for the selection and assignment of stories, *editorial writers* who write articles to indicate the opinion of the paper on issues and events, and *copy editors* who process the copy for publication.

Newspaper advertising departments employ people in the classified and display advertisement departments. Both use *copy writers, salespersons, advertising managers,* and *national representatives*.

Production department personnel select materials and suppliers for the printing of the newspaper; they may also supervise in-house printing. Jobs here range from *production assistant* (or *traffic assistant*) to *production manager* or *production director*.

Circulation departments, which are responsible for the distribution of the paper, employ *circulation assistants, collection managers,* and *circulation managers* of different ranks.

## Wire Services and Syndicates

Wire services, popularly known as the wholesalers of news, have traditionally been happy hunting grounds for people seeking entry into the world of journalism. Many people start out as stringers for Associated Press or United Press International, the nation's leading wire services. Such stringers often go on to serve as correspondents and bureau chiefs, both at home and abroad. Although most of the foreign bureaus of the wire services are headed by Americans, most of their reporters, copy readers, rewrites, correspondents, researchers, photographers, and photo editors are hired from the respective countries.

Syndicates provide features, columns, cartoon panels, and comic strips to newspapers and magazines; they require the talent of experienced journalists. About a dozen major syndicates and over 100 smaller ones supply packaged entertainment and educational material.

## Magazines

The magazine industry provides interesting and rather lucrative jobs for thousands of people looking for an alternative to the daily pressure and rigor of newspaper journalism. Magazines provide more room for creativity for writers, editors, and artists. There are at least 10,800 magazines and 9,000 industrial and company publications (internal or external) in the United States.

Magazines employ editors of different grade levels. The entry-level position is that of the *editorial assistant* or *researcher. Assistant editor, associate editor, senior editor,* and *executive* or *managing editor* follow. These people are responsible for selecting and processing the content of the magazine. They review manuscripts and assign stories based on ideas they have developed. On small magazines, they also serve as rewrites and copy editors. *Staff writers, art directors,* and *photographers* are also key links in the editorial chain.

Magazine advertising departments offer positions of *sales assistant, sales representative, sales manager,* and *advertising manager.* This department makes or breaks the magazine, whose major source of income is advertising; the profit from sale of copies is marginal. A successful magazine is expected to break even through advertising sales alone.

Magazine circulation departments attract enterprising people who are willing to start as *circulation assistants* and hope to go on to become *managers of collection, assistant directors of circulation,* and eventually *circulation managers.*

Magazine production involves the services of *art directors, photoengravers, typesetters, press operators,* and supervisory personnel such as *production managers* and *layout coordinators.*

The business or administrative structure of major magazines calls for other positions such as *promotion director, business manager, director of administration, general manager,* and *publishers.* Some magazines have a separate operations department.

## Broadcast Journalism

For years, radio stations in the United States were not allowed to carry news. Today, radio and television have become the main source of news for the majority of the population. Although entertainment continues to be their main function, the broadcast media have been increasing their news output, especially through the introduction of the all-news format. Most of the 4,649 FM and 4,733 AM radio stations and the 539 VHF and 357 UHF television stations in operation in this country devote at least some of their airtime to news coverage. Additionally, they carry news features, documentaries, and interviews, all of which require the services of journalists.

The growth of broadcast journalism in the United States has created a steady increase of jobs for journalists. The electronic media hire *reporters, announcers, newscasters, news writers, news directors,* and *producers* of news programs and features. Three major commercial networks and the Public Broadcasting Service (PBS) with its 303 affiliates continue to be the main employers in this field. The advent of cable television has opened more jobs at the local level, but most of the 6,200 U.S. cable systems have limited news staff on their payrolls.

**Business Journalism**     Business and industry employ writers and journalists to work on internal and external newsletters, press releases issued by the public relations department, maintenance and operation manuals. Writers and journalists also work with scientists, engineers, and executives in preparing scientific and trade journal articles.

## JOB DESCRIPTIONS: NEWSPAPERS

**News department.**    The news or reporting department consists of reporters, writers, and photographers. The entry-level job involves research, filing, moving the copy, rewriting press releases, and writing simple stories (such as community events and obituaries). At some small-circulation papers, *news assistants* are also given the responsibility of reporting meetings and community events. *Beat reporters* cover specific places, such as police headquarters and city hall. *General assignment reporters* and more experienced *staff reporters* cover major local events and events of national importance. The proven reporters are assigned investigative reporting assignments. *Critics* and *columnists* complete the news team.

*Rewrites* are writers who rewrite stories phoned in by staff reporters or filed by wire services. They have to be distinguished from *staff writers,* who are in fact reporters in small-circulation newspapers.

*Photographers* are not second-class citizens in the newsroom; they get the same salary scale as the reporters and are considered an important part of the news gathering team. Experienced photographers sometimes even direct the work of less-experienced reporters with whom they team up for assignments.

**Editing department.**    The editing department is headed by the *managing editor,* under whom work the *city editor, news editor,* and *section editors,* who handle sections such as sports, business, and lifestyle. Reporters and photographers work directly under the city editor, while *copy editors* work under the news editor. The *editorial page editor* and her or his team of writers are an independent unit that works parallel to the managing editor.

Copy editors prepare copy for publication by correcting factual, linguistic, and legal errors; they also write headlines. It is often easier to obtain a job as copy editor than as a reporter or writer. Copy desk is the best training ground for future reporters and writers.

**Advertising department.**    The advertising department consists of *account executives, advertising managers,* and *advertising director.* Most advertising beginners start in the classified department and move on to the display department. They assist the senior sales personnel who handle accounts. In large-circulation newspapers, there are specialized advertising managers for client categories, such as automobiles, real estate, and retail sales. More experienced executives handle national accounts.

**Production department.**   Production departments offer job opportunities for creative, mechanical, and administrative talent. Composition of newspapers is a specialized job, even in these days of computerized typesetting and page makeup. *Photoengravers* prepare photographs for printing. *Printers* work on the printing machinery in the pressroom. For most medium-sized daily newspapers, the pressroom and composing room are separate operations.

**Circulation department.**   Circulation departments market the newspaper to the public. People with business skills can find employment in this branch without much difficulty. Personnel in this department are responsible for customer relations and for increasing circulation. They also supervise the delivery staff. The entry-level position is *district manager*. Considerable market research and labor management responsibilities are attached to this job.

**Education: Newspapers**

Entry-level positions in the news department often call for a college degree. More than 300 universities and colleges in the United States offer journalism education (a list of the departments and schools accredited by the Association for Education in Journalism and Mass Communication is provided at the end of this chapter). Ability both to type and to use computer terminals are required qualifications for the reporting and editorial staff of most newspapers. Superior linguistic and writing ability and the ability to work under pressure and tight deadlines are desirable qualities for reporters. Photographers are trained at schools of journalism or fine arts or at other institutes of photography.

Advertising, circulation, and business departments of newspapers seek college graduates for entry-level positions. A degree in journalism or business-related areas is desirable. Good interpersonal communication skills and telephone etiquette are essential. Familiarity with advertising and retail business will be of great advantage for job seekers in these areas.

The production department is usually staffed by people who have acquired their skills through apprenticeships in composing, printing, or photoengraving. Trade schools and institutes offer training in these crafts. Basic knowledge of journalism acquired in high school education is a great asset for these technical and artistic people, as it enables them to do their jobs more meaningfully.

**Experience: Newspapers**

The best way to obtain an entry-level job in newspapers is to participate in an *internship* during your college career. Many companies hire their promising interns. Experience on the college newspaper and other college publications is another major resource for a person wishing to enter the profession. As a college graduate, you could be hired as *news assist-*

*ant* by a major newspaper and as a *reporter* or *staff writer* in a small newspaper. After two or three years, you could be promoted as reporter of a medium-sized newspaper. Three to six years in that capacity will make you eligible for a position as reporter for a major newspaper or *section editor* or *city editor* for a medium-sized newspaper. You could even become the editor of a small paper at that stage. At least 10–15 years in the field of journalism are required for an editorial position in a major metropolitan newspaper.

*Copy editors* with three to five years of experience may be promoted to positions as reporters or *staff writers. Department editors* are promoted from the ranks of writers and reporters. *Editorial page editors* are carefully chosen from experienced staff members who are loyal to the philosophies and goals of the newspaper management.

In advertising, a college degree is required for an entry-level position at a small newspaper. One or two years at a small paper will be required to obtain a similar position in a medium or large-sized metropolitan daily. Five to six years of experience could bring you the position of *advertising manager* in a small or medium-sized newspaper, while seven to ten years will be required for a comparable position in a large metropolitan daily. The top job in the hierarchy is that of *advertising director,* which calls for at least ten years' experience at a small or medium-sized paper and well over 15 years at a major metropolitan daily.

Most jobs in the production department require hands-on experience, through apprenticeships in a newspaper establishment or experience in related industries (such as printing and publishing). Promotion to supervisory positions is based on technical skills and experience within the organization.

If you are interested in working in the circulation department of a newspaper, a college degree could earn you the entry-level position of *district manager. Branch managers* and *circulation directors* require up to 10 years and 15 years of experience, respectively.

## JOB DESCRIPTIONS: WIRE SERVICES AND SYNDICATES

The first job in wire services is that of *stringer.* This is a part-time position taken by many students who want to gain experience before seeking a reporting or editing job at a newspaper or magazine. The full-time position at the entry level is that of *editorial assistant.* That job often consists of rewriting routine stories from local newspapers and gathering information and verifying facts over the phone.

*Reporters, copy editors, rewrites,* and *photographers* for wire services and syndicates perform almost the same function as their counterparts in the newspaper organization and enjoy the same status. After several years in the capacity of *editor* or *reporter,* some are promoted as *bureau chiefs* at small or medium-sized bureaus. *Foreign correspondents* are the stars of the wire service world.

**Education: Wire Services and Syndicates**

The qualifications for wire service personnel are almost the same as those for newspapers. Entry-level positions require a college degree. The nature of the job involves assignments all over the U.S. and abroad. Deadline pressure is much greater on wire service personnel than on newspaper staff members who may have one major deadline a day. Wire service staff members should be more aggressive, fast, accurate, and concise. They should be able to make quick decisions under pressing circumstances. Writing and editing skills of high quality are expected, and ability to write extremely quickly will be a major asset, as there is more editing and rewriting than reporting involved in this work.

**Experience: Wire Services and Syndicates**

Turnover of personnel is very high at a wire service, as many journalists use it as a training ground for a newspaper or magazine job. The wire services are known for their willingness to hire recent college graduates and inexperienced people. Often, new employees may find themselves in charge of late shifts, performing almost all the journalistic functions possible.

Five to ten years of experience is required for promotion to a small or medium-size bureau. Foreign correspondents and bureau chiefs are required to work in the New York or Washington D.C. bureaus before an overseas assignment. Advancement slows with years in the agency; that seems to be one of the reasons for the high turnover.

### JOB DESCRIPTIONS: MAGAZINES

**Editing.**   The entry-level magazine job is that of an *editorial assistant* or *researcher*. The tasks assigned to the beginner are not very exciting or creative. Routine duties such as answering the telephone, typing manuscripts and correspondence, contacting writers on the phone, and filing must be expected. In smaller magazines, some amount of rewriting, copy editing, proofreading, and even writing of tidbits are assigned to the novice.

At the level of *assistant editor,* more writing and editing will be involved. Assistant editors are able to write in areas of their specialty and interest. They also discuss story ideas with writers and work with them. Some work with art directors and printers may also be involved in small or medium-sized magazines.

*Associate editors* and *senior editors* do less writing and more editing and rewriting. They work closely with the writers of major stories. Senior editors are in charge of the editing of specific sections of the magazine.

The top position of *executive editor, managing editor,* or *editor-in-chief* involves the overall administration of the magazine. In small magazines, these positions are combined with that of the senior editor.

Business and trade magazines, published by organizations for internal and external publicity, are edited by comparatively small staffs. In many cases, it is a one-person operation with some clerical help. The editing of an organization's magazine or newsletter is only one of the many tasks assigned to *director of media relations* or public relations personnel. In recent years, many so-called "house organs" have become quite sophisticated in content and appearance, and more resources and staff have been assigned to them. People with all-round editing, writing, and production skills will find this kind of operation exciting and rewarding.

**Advertising.** Magazines hire *sales assistants* (or *sales trainees*) in their advertising departments. This position is mainly clerical, with work like answering the telephones, typing letters, and filing. Research on clients and their products and helping senior personnel prepare for meetings and accompanying them to some of the presentations are creative tasks often available at this level only in small magazines.

Many sales representatives work with advertising agencies that represent individual advertisers. Direct contact with the advertisers takes place only for classified ads and some local ads. *Group sales managers* deal almost exclusively with ad agencies. The *director of advertising* is responsible for developing permanent clients for the magazine.

**Production.** Most magazines do not have in-house printing facilities; hence, the work of the magazine production department is less technical and more administrative. The beginner in the profession is appointed as *production assistant* or *traffic assistant*. Production assistants do typing, filing, and the dummy file. Traffic assistants manage the flow of layout and proofs, and keep track of production schedules; they also do some work with the printer and suppliers. *Layout coordinators* are responsible for supervising the layout and printing process, while *production managers* arrange contracts, prepare the schedules, and negotiate the budgets. The entire operation is supervised by the *production director.*

**Circulation.** *Circulation assistants* perform duties similar to editorial or advertising assistants. They also handle subscriber complaints. The *manager of collections* and renewals has the responsibility of maintaining the current subscriber base, especially through creative and persuasive direct-mail marketing. The *assistant director of circulation* is entrusted with the task of increasing circulation through mail and newsstand sales. The *circulation director* oversees both these operations.

**Education: Magazines**

Most facets of magazine work involve writing and creative abilities. Formal training in magazine journalism, offered by several colleges and universities will be a major asset for beginners. Many institutions offer short programs in magazine writing, production, and publishing through their schools of continuing education and summer workshops. The most basic skills are writing, interviewing, and editing.

Entry-level positions in the editorial department of magazines require good linguistic skills and creative ideas. A typing speed of at least 40 words per minute is a must; experience in the use of computer terminals or word processors may be required. Basic knowledge of the printing and production procedures is desirable.

Assistant editors and associate editors must have proven writing and copy editing abilities. They should be able to generate story ideas and be proficient in current trends and developments. Good proofreading ability is an additional asset.

Senior editors should have excellent negotiation skills, as they have to deal with literary agents and writers. A sound knowledge of copyright laws and other legal issues related to publishing is also important for a senior editor. The editor-in-chief or managing editor should have strong administrative skills in addition to editorial and creative talent.

People who work on professional journals, such as medical or business periodicals, need considerable knowledge of the journal's subject. Technical writing also requires the ability to write for the average casual reader.

Personnel of company or house journals should have sound knowledge of the goals of the organization and be loyal to its policies. They should be experts in proactive rather than reactive journalism, as their main function is image- and morale-building rather than investigative and objective reporting of information.

A degree in advertising or business management could be very useful for entry-level employees of the advertising department. Some business experience, basic secretarial skills, and good phone manners are basic requirements. The circulation and promotion departments call for identical skills; magazines seem to prefer graduates in business administration or marketing for these operations. Basic computing skills also become very handy in these departments.

The production department looks for people with good business skills and creative training. Many institutes offer programs in photography, layout and design, and magazine publishing and production. Apprenticeships in these trades are valuable training grounds for these jobs. Basic copy editing skills and excellent proofreading skills as well as some business experience are additional assets to the employees of this department.

**Experience: Magazines**

For entry-level positions in the editorial department, a magazine internship experience is the best qualification. Experience on college magazines and newsletters is also helpful. Two or three years as editorial assistant may lead to a promotion as assistant editor in a medium-sized magazine. On a large magazine, the wait will be longer. Many small magazines and trade and industry journals employ recent college graduates as assistant editors and promote the proven ones to the position of associate editor in a year or two. Almost ten years of experience is required for promotion to senior editor in most medium-sized magazines. Higher editorial positions require a successful track record and a few more years of experience.

A college degree and basic clerical skills will earn you an entry-level position in the advertising department. The move to the position of sales representative may need three years' experience, and it will take another three or so for the job of group sales manager. Advertising managers come from the ranks of people who have invested at least ten years in the business.

Recent graduates who are hired as circulation assistants have to prove themselves for three to five years before becoming collection or renewal managers. If things work well, experience gained in another couple of years could lead to the position of assistant director of circulation. The top job, that of the circulation manager or director, requires almost ten years experience in the field.

The move from the position of production or traffic assistant in the production department may be rather fast for a recent college graduate; in a year or two, you could become a layout coordinator. The next move, to the position of production manager, could be a good ten years away, on a medium-sized or large magazine. The end-of-the-line job of production director involves a shorter wait for a good production manager.

An experienced and successful advertising director or editor could eventually become the publisher of the magazine. This move, like the promotions in most departments of the magazine establishment, depends mostly on the size of the publication.

## JOB DESCRIPTIONS: BROADCAST JOURNALISM

Broadcast journalism is one of the most competitive career areas in mass communication. Most jobs go to insiders, and the road to the top is narrow and long. The competition for on-the-air jobs is much more intense than for the behind-the-scene jobs.

**Radio.**    In radio, most beginners start as *desk assistants* or *news assistants* at network stations. Their duties include answering the telephones, some amount of clerical work, basic research, filing, phone calls for verification of information, and even rewriting of small, routine stories.

*Reporters* gather news and record events on tape. Some technical skills and good reporting, writing, and speaking ability are required. Reporters work under tremendous deadline pressure. Most of them start as reporters for small network or independent stations and move on as reporters of a major market. The last step on the reporting ladder is that of *network reporter.*

Large stations employ *newswriters* and *editors* who prepare copy for the *announcers*. *Newscasters* are on-air personalities who get maximum public exposure. The reporters share part of it when their words are recorded as part of the "cuts." Newscasters at many stations are also required to write at least part of the newscast.

Reporters are promoted to the position of *news director*, responsible for the news operation of the station or network. The position of news director is the dream of many broadcast journalists.

**Television.** In television, desk assistants perform almost identical duties as desk assistants in radio. At major stations, they keep files, take care of the wire copies that come on telex lines, as well as serve as messengers. They may be asked to check facts by telephone for reporters and writers. At small stations, they rewrite wire copy and review film clippings.

*Newswriters* handle the responsibility of preparing the newscasts, while *correspondents* or reporters go to the field and gather news with the assistance of the camera crew. The emphasis on "live" telecasts has increased the importance of their work, as well as its pressures. *Newseditors* also edit copy submitted by reporters.

The *assistant news producers* help the *news producer* assign stories and select them in the order of priority for the newscast. They also oversee routine production operations. Again, the position of the news director is the ultimate career goal of most behind-the-scene broadcast journalists.

The stars of television journalism are the *anchor persons* of newscasts and news magazines such as *60 Minutes*. The anchor person and the reporters are seen on the screen by the viewing public. Network anchor is one of the most coveted positions in the communications industry.

**Education: Broadcast Journalism**

Hundreds of colleges and universities impart education in broadcast journalism. Some of the radio and television institutes also offer short-term courses in it. College radio and television stations continue to be major training grounds for aspiring broadcast journalists.

A career in radio requires good voice quality. One must command considerable self-confidence and learn voice control techniques to go on the air as a newscaster or reporter. Knowledge of basic production techniques is a must for reporters and newscasters.

Writers and reporters should have good writing skills and the ability to handle deadline pressure. On-the-spot reporting also requires a great degree of courage and a spirit of adventure as one often has to physically push oneself to get close to events and people. Good interviewing skills are the lifeblood of a good broadcast journalist.

On-camera jobs in television require pleasing on-air appearance or screen personality. Confidence and ability for improvisation are expected of reporters and newscasters, especially when they are on camera live. Fluency of speech and a good command of the language prove critical to their success. A successful anchor will also be a good newswriter and interviewer.

**Experience: Broadcast Journalism**

Experience is the most crucial ingredient of a job search in broadcasting due to strong competition. Most jobs are not advertised; insiders who have been working their way up earn them.

In radio and in television, beginners often start in small stations outside metropolitan areas and after gaining substantial experience move to metropolitan stations and network stations. This pattern of job mobility is frequent both in radio and television.

College graduates who enter radio journalism as desk assistants at network stations or reporters at small network stations serve in those capacities before becoming reporters in medium-sized stations. A few years as a reporter at a major station or news director at a small station lead to the position of network reporter or news director.

## SOURCES OF INFORMATION

**Associations and Societies**

Addresses for these associations and societies are provided in the appendix.

American Newspaper Publishers Association
American Society of Magazine Editors
American Society of Newspaper Editors
Associated Press Broadcasters Inc.
Association of National Advertisers, Inc.
InterAmerican Press Association
International Circulation Managers Association
International Federation of Newspaper Publishers
Investigative Reporters and Editors, Inc.
Magazine Publishers Association
National Association of Broadcasters
National Association of Science Writers
National Conference of Editorial Writers
National Newspaper Association
National Press Photographers Association
Newspaper Advertising Bureau, Inc.
Newspaper Guild, The
Radio-Television News Directors Association
Society of National Association Publications
Southern Newspaper Publishers Association, Inc.
Suburban Newspapers of America
Society of Professional Journalists (Sigma Delta Chi)

## RECOMMENDED READING

**News Reporting and Writing**

Brooks, Brian, George Kennedy, Daryl Moen, and Don Ranly. *News Reporting and Writing*. 2nd ed. New York: St. Martin's Press, 1985.

Hough, George E. *Newswriting*. 4th ed. Boston: Houghton Mifflin, 1988.

Mencher, Melvin. *News Reporting and Writing*. 5th ed. Dubuque, IA: Wm. C. Brown, 1991.

*Specialized Reporting*

Gaines, William. *Investigative Reporting for Print and Broadcast*. Chicago: Nelson-Hall, 1992.

Meyer, Philip. *Precision Journalism: A Reporter's Introduction to Social Science Methods*. 2nd ed. Bloomington: University of Indiana Press.

*Editorial and Opinion Writing*

Stonecipher, Harry W. *Editorial and Persuasive Writing*. New York: Hastings House, 1990.

*Copy Editing*

Baskette, Floyd, Jack Z. Sissors, and Brian S. Brooks. *The Art of Editing*. 4th ed. New York: Macmillan, 1993.

Garst, Robert E. and Theodore Bernstein. *Headlines and Deadlines: A Manual for Copy Editors*. New York: Columbia University Press, 1982.

*Magazine*

Click, J. W. *Magazine Editing and Production*. 5th ed. Dubuque, IA: Wm. C. Brown, 1990.

Mogel, Leonard, *The Magazine: Everything You Need to Know to Make it in the Magazine Business*. 3rd ed. Englewood Cliffs, NJ: Prentice-Hall, 1992.

*Broadcast Journalism*

Bliss, Edward and John M. Patterson. *Writing News for Broadcast*. New York: Columbia University Press, 1978.

Stephens, Mitchell. *Broadcast News: Radio Journalism and an Introduction to Television*. 3rd ed. Fort Worth, TX: Harcourt Brace, 1993.

## PERIODICALS

Addresses for the following periodicals of interest can be found in Appendix B.

*Columbia Journalism Review*
*Editor and Publisher*
*Folio: The Magazine of Magazine Management*
*Journal of Communication*

*Journalism History*
*Journalism Quarterly*
*Magazine and Bookseller*
*Masthead*
*Public Opinion Quarterly*
*Washington Journalism Review*

**Directories**

*Ayer Directory of Publications.* Philadelphia: Ayer Press. Annual.

*Broadcasting Weekly—Yearbook Issue.* Washington, DC: Broadcasting Publications, Inc. Annual.

*Editor and Publisher International Year Book.* New York: Editor and Publishers Company, Inc. Annual.

*Television Factbook.* Washington, DC: Television Digest, Inc. Annual.

*Writer's Market: Where to Sell What You Write.* Cincinnati, OH: Writer's Digest Books. Annual.

## SCHOLARSHIPS

*Journalism Career and Scholarship Guide,* prepared by The Dow Jones Newspaper Fund Inc., P.O. Box 300, Princeton, N.J. 08540 is the best source of information. It lists national scholarships as well as fellowships and scholarships offered by leading universities and colleges.

American Newspaper Publishers
   Foundation
The Newspaper Center
P.O. Box 17407, Dulles
   International Airport
Washington, DC 20041

American Press Institute
11690 Sunrise Valley Drive
Reston, VA 22091

Dow Jones Newspaper Fund Inc.
P.O. Box 300
Princeton, NJ 08543

Gannet Foundation
Lincoln Tower
Rochester, NY 14604

William Randolph Hearst
   Foundation
609 Market Street, Suite 502
San Francisco, CA 94104

InterAmerican Press Association
   Scholarship Fund Inc.
2911 NW 39th Street
Miami, FL 33142

Nieman Foundation
One Francis Ave
Cambridge, MA 02138

Pulliam Journalism Fellowship
P.O. Box 145
Indianapolis, IN 46206

Reader's Digest Foundation
Pleasantville, NY 10570

Scripps-Howard Foundation
1100 Central Trust Tower
Cincinnati, OH 45202

Sigma Delta Chi Foundation
53 W. Jackson Blvd., Suite 731
Chicago, IL 60604

## ACCREDITED COLLEGES AND UNIVERSITIES

The journalism sequences of the following colleges and universities have been accredited by the Association for Education in Journalism and Mass Communication (AEJMC). Additional accreditations may have been awarded by the time you are ready to make your selection, and you should contact AEJMC for the most recent list.

American University
Arizona State University
Arkansas State University
Ball State University
Bowling Green State University
Brigham Young University
California State University–
  Fresno
California State University–
  Fullerton
California State University–
  Long Beach
California State University–
  Northridge
Colorado State University
Columbia University
Drake University
Eastern Illinois University
Florida A&M University
Humboldt State University
Indiana University
Iowa State University
Jackson State University
Kansas State University
Kent State University
Louisiana State University
Marshall University
Memphis State University
Michigan State University
New York University
North Texas State University
Northern Illinois University
Ohio State University
Oklahoma State University
Pennsylvania State University
San Diego State University
San Francisco State University
San Jose State University

South Dakota State University
Southern Illinois University–
  Carbondale
Southern Illinois University–
  Edwardsville
St. Cloud State University
Syracuse University
Temple University
Texas A&M University
Texas Christian University
Texas Tech University
University of Alabama
University of Alaska–Fairbanks
University of Arizona
University of Arkansas–
  Fayetteville
University of Arkansas–
  Little Rock
University of California–Berkeley
University of Colorado
University of Florida
University of Georgia
University of Hawaii
University of Illinois–
  Urbana–Champaign
University of Iowa
University of Kansas
University of Kentucky
University of Maryland
University of Minnesota
University of Mississippi
University of Missouri
University of Montana
University of Nebraska–Lincoln
University of Nevada
University of New Mexico
University of North Carolina–
  Chapel Hill

University of North Dakota
University of Ohio
University of Oklahoma
University of Oregon
University of Rhode Island
University of South Carolina
University of South Florida
University of Southern California
University of Tennessee–Knoxville
University of Texas–Austin
University of Utah
University of Washington

University of West Virginia
University of Wisconsin–
  Eau Claire
University of Wisconsin–Madison
University of Wisconsin–Oshkosh
University of Wisconsin–
  River Falls
Virginia Commonwealth
  University
Washington and Lee University
Western Kentucky University

The broadcast journalism sequences of the following colleges and universities have been accredited by the Association for Education in Journalism and Mass Communication (AEJMC):

American University
Bowling Green State University
Brigham Young University
Colorado State University
Florida A&M University
Indiana University
Iowa State University
Jackson State University
Louisiana State University
Marshall University
Memphis State University
New York University
Ohio State University
San Jose State University
Syracuse University

University of Alaska–Fairbanks
University of California–Berkeley
University of Illinois–
  Urbana–Champaign
University of Minnesota
University of Missouri
University of Ohio
University of Oregon
University of Texas–Austin
University of Utah
University of Washington
University of West Virginia
University of Wisconsin–Madison
Virginia Commonwealth
  University

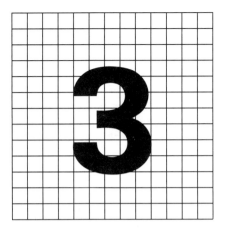

# PHOTOGRAPHY

Photography is a unique profession. Friends and potential competitors alike freely share their knowledge with the newcomer. Few other professions offer such willing help to people just entering the field.

Berwin Johnson, Robert E. Mayer and Fred Schmidt, *Opportunities in Photography Careers* (Lincolnwood, IL: VGM Career Horizons, 1991).

A career in photography is one of the most satisfying careers a person can have. But don't be misled. If you are interested in photography only for the money, for the glamour, or purely as an art form—be careful and cautious in your planning.

*Money:* Many professions and crafts pay a great deal more and require less work than photography. While many professional photographers live comfortably, own their own homes, send their children to college, and are respected in their communities, few are in a high income bracket.

*Glamour:* It is true that, to the general public, being a photographer has an air of glamour about it. And it *is* glamorous, in a way. Once in a while, you hear of a photographer who is a member of the jet set, but very few photographers get to photograph the beautiful people or travel to exotic places in the line of duty.

*Art:* Photography as an art form has gained recognition and acceptance—not bad for a technology that has been around less than 150 years. However, very few photographers make a living at selling their photographs as art or as collectibles.

The good news is this: if you sincerely want to be a photographer, to satisfy a need (that of your client) or to help understand or to communicate better—especially if you want to get into photography because of the challenge that being a photographer offers—you'll have little trouble making a success of your efforts, provided you have the ability, the business acumen, and the strong desire necessary to become a professional photographer.

Actually, getting into photography is easy. All you really need is access to a telephone, a business card, some equipment, and credit at a photo lab. Getting into photography is one thing; staying in it is quite another.

Photography is one of the few remaining art/crafts, in which entrepreneurs can develop at their own pace. A formal education isn't necessary, although chances are that a person who has a formal degree will have a better chance at succeeding than one who does not.

A large number of colleges and universities offer courses in photography, and a large number of students are taking these courses. Many of these students aspire to get into photography. As a consequence, only the most talented, most aggressive will earn, and keep, the top spots. The competition is fierce. Not only are the new graduates trying to enter the marketplace, so are people (of all ages) from other disciplines. In addition, America is the focal point of the world for this art and craft. Consequently, students and photographers from every part of the planet come here to seek their fortunes.

### THE JOBS

Professional photography, truly a service industry, is thought of in four categories: portraiture, commercial–illustration photography, photojournalism, and industrial photography. Nearly everyone who earns a living as a photographer will probably fit into one of these general classifications. There is crossover among the four disciplines, and within each are subdivisions and levels of activities.

**Portraiture**

The readily entered segment of professional photography is portraiture, making pictures of people. Many different types of portraits are made by many different types of photographers and studios. There are as many different styles of portraiture as there are portraitists.

**Record photography.**   The simple, structured, record-type of portraiture can be found in shopping centers and in department stores (like Sears, J.C. Penney's, and K-Mart). Such photography is of children and family groups. The poses are straightforward, the lighting is standard and preset, and the number of poses is limited. Unquestionably, this type of photography offers the consumer the best value for money. The photography is "clean"; the resulting prints are of good quality and good color, and provide an adequate record of the people pictured.

Working in one of these studios is a good entry-level job. It provides good experience in dealing with the public in a studio atmosphere and an opportunity to make photographs in the real world.

**Family photography.**   The majority of portrait studios across the United States are at the next level. The average studio specializes in the portraiture of children and family groups, plus babies and adults of all ages. The photographer offers a variety of "documentary" poses and arrangements, perhaps including props and accessories. Sometimes makeup is applied to hide skin blemishes. Lighting is carefully placed to complement the individual or individuals being photographed. Some studios have a garden or outdoor setting.

This kind of studio offers a wide choice of poses and generally provides larger prints than the record-type businesses, although small sizes are also available. The large prints are delivered in moderate to expensive frames for placement in the home or office. The prices charged are relative to the quality of the work produced.

Sizes of these studios range from small to large. They are usually family owned and operated, although some belong to large photography companies. Some of these studios also specialize in the portraiture of high school seniors, which can be important to the bottom line. Most of the businesses depend upon the photography of weddings (and brides) for a substantial part of their income.

Working in one of these places of business usually requires some experience. A job as an assistant cameraperson, a finisher (matting and framing), or salesperson for example, would require previous experience. However, some photographers will train an entry-level person who shows promise. Apprenticeship of a good beginner with an experienced photographer can benefit both the studio and the beginner.

Personal attributes necessary for portraiture work include an ability to deal well with co-workers, skill in working with the public, and a pleasant personality. Willingness to follow the suggested dress code and to take direction are necessary, as well as adaptability in learning the particular style of portraiture offered. A knowledge of photography, particularly lighting and posing, is essential.

**Custom photography.**   At the top, quality and price wise, is the custom portrait studio. The studios in this relatively small group are usually small enterprises as businesses go, run by one, two, or three people—often a photographer and her or his spouse, with the spouse acting as business manager, salesperson, and even retoucher. The photographs produced by this type of studio are true works of art; the matting and framing are of the best quality. A few studios offer dye transfer photographic prints, the ultimate in quality. Print sizes vary, the largest being $40'' \times 60''$. Interpretive portraits made by custom studios are the potential heirlooms of tomorrow. Custom studios also make fine executive portraits that find their way into corporate annual reports, as well as to the spot above the fireplace at home.

When James R. Israel was head of the portrait studio at General Motors Corporation, his photograph of the chairman of the board of GM was the first nonpainting to hang in the GM boardroom.

One of America's leading portraitists is Christopher DerManuelian, who also specializes in architecture and sophisticated wedding photography. He owns a one-person business in San Mateo, California. He learns as much as he can about his subject, even visiting the room where the photograph will be displayed so he can complement the environment with the portrait. Christopher studied civil engineering in Beirut, Lebanon, and completed his studies in the United States. He entered his new profession with little preparation. He says, "When you do your best, sooner or later people will come to recognize and appreciate your work."

In the majority of studios for all three types of portraiture described, the processing and printing are finished by outside professional laboratories. However, with the advent of one-hour "mini-labs," some studios do their own photofinishing, sometimes in cooperation with other local studios. Matting, framing, and packaging are usually done by the individual studios.

**Commercial–Illustration Photography**

Portraiture involves a somewhat narrow range of photographic opportunities; commercial–illustration photography, by contrast, includes a wide variety of specialties. A commercial studio may offer photography for many different purposes, or it may specialize in only a few types. For the most part, these studios produce photographs for advertising, annual reports, brochures, catalogs, editorial use, packaging, and promotion and public relations. Although most commercial–illustration photographic work is published in some form, prints and transparencies are also used for convention exhibit displays, point-of-purchase (POP) displays, sales meetings, sales presentations, wall decor, and window displays.

*Commercial photography* is used to document manufacturing processes and illustrate products, from computer chips to nuts-and-bolts to glassware to aircraft. *Architectural photography* is a specialty, as is *aerial photography. Illustration photography* appears in magazines and newspapers, depicting people, places, and products.

A popular medium in commercial photography, other than the photographic print, is the 35mm transparency for multi-image presentations. These can be as simple as a one-projector slide show for speaker support, or as complex as a program using many projectors showing hundreds of slides in a relatively short time on a large screen before a large audience. Multi-image shows are commonly presented at sales meetings, fairs, exhibitions, and theme parks.

Commercial–illustration studios can be small studios for still-lifes only, with one or two people. A medium-sized studio might have a drive-in bay and one or two additional smaller studios, with six or eight employees. The largest photographic companies, such as Kranzten in Chicago, occupy multi-story buildings in several locations; dozens of people fill a variety of jobs: stylists and home economists, photographers and assistant photographers, laboratory technicians, salespeople, and office staff.

Few commercial studios are located in small towns; most are located where manufacturing and light industry plants support the area. A good place to seek employment is in any major league baseball city, as these cities tend to have not only manufacturing and service industries, but also advertising and public relations agencies that use photography on a regular basis. Although New York is the center of such activity, a look at one issue of *Photo/Design* magazine shows display ads from photo-illustrators in Hillsboro, Oregon; Nashville, Tennessee; Baltimore, Maryland; Mannheim, Pennsylvania; Birmingham, Alabama; and Los Angeles, California.

The 35mm transparency has caused a technique to become an industry. Producing slide/sound programs for presentation to the business-industrial community, as well as to the public, is akin to producing a film or television production, except the medium is slides and recorded sound. Special skills are needed in the photography, scripting, programming and projection of a multi-image show. The group that represents those who work in this medium is the Association for Multi-Image International.

The association for commercial illustrators is the Advertising Photographers of America, which has affiliated groups in New York, Chicago, and Los Angeles. *Photo District News* annually sponsors two conferences of professional photographers, one in New York and one in Los Angeles.

Personal attributes essential to a commercial photographer are self-motivation, dependability, business acumen, and the ability to get along with others. Most assignments have rigid deadlines; the ability to provide speedy and dependable service is crucial.

## Photojournalism

Photojournalism is performed primarily by independent freelance entrepreneurs who are in the business of taking pictures for publication. Photojournalists also make photographs for publicity and for multi-image presentations. They usually specialize in two or three fields, such as agriculture, annual reports, business and industry, personalities, or travel.

A prime source of income for many freelance photojournalists is stock photography. The photojournalist turns over transparencies by the thousands to picture agencies. The images on file are of every conceivable subject or situation, and are used in textbooks, encyclopedias, annual reports, magazines, etc. The picture agency (or "stock house") has exclusive rights to the images in its files and pays the photographer a percentage of the fee paid each time a picture is used. This way it is possible for one slide (which is replicated) to earn thousands of dollars for the photographer.

Though the field of photojournalism is small and rather limited, there are opportunities for editors, librarians, and picture researchers. An organization devoted to this aspect of photography is the American Society of Picture Professionals. The lives of photojournalists are interesting and varied.

Travel photographer Charles A. Weckler, an independent businessman, based in Hawaii, travels the world updating his stock file which is managed by his wife, Cindy Weckler. Mr. Weckler also works for clients directly, producing photographs for advertising and editorial use. Bill Rivelli, working out of his studio in New York, specializes in business and industry photos; Bill's wife, Cynthia Rivelli, is his agent and manages the business of Rivelli Photography, Inc. Kay Reese, who owns Kay Reese & Associates Inc., "Corporate photography worldwide," has offices in the historic Flatiron building in the heart of New York's photo district; Kay is agent for a group of photographers who travel the world on assignments for editorial and advertising purposes.

Award-winning newspaper photographer Bill Strode once said, "I tackle my routine assignments as if they were of national importance." Arthur Rothstein, photographer of the famous "Oklahoma Dust Storm" and many other pictures of that era, observed, "Photojournalists are the observers of people and events who report what's happening in photographs, interpreters of facts who write with a camera." Rothstein went on to become chief photographer for *Look* magazine and then to a new career with *Parade*. Annie Liebovitz of *Rolling Stone* fame is a well-known photographer of people and events, carrying on a tradition of women in photography, which began with Julia Margaret Cameron in the nineteenth century.

Many photojournalists and television news camerapeople belong to the National Press Photographers Association. They subscribe to *News Photographer* magazine and attend the NPPA's annual conference and NPPA-sponsored short courses.

The book *A Day in the Life of America* shows how photojournalists from around the world can work together to compile an important record of a nation. This book is an excellent example of the best in today's photo-reportage.

Working as an employee for or on retainer from a magazine or newspaper or wire service can be an exciting and rewarding career, taking pictures of events as they occur and the aftermath or follow-up events. Competition with other photographers is ever present; one can expect a bit of "jostling" at important news events. To be a news photojournalist, the photographer must be strong enough physically to carry heavy equipment (photojournalists are the "pack horses" of the industry) and be ready and willing to go anywhere at a moment's notice. The photographer must always be alert and have the stamina for rigorous, and even dangerous, assignments.

A degree in liberal arts, with courses in anthropology and human relations would be beneficial in this work.

## Industrial Photography

The list of past winners of the Nikon Industrial Photographer of the Year Award, and the companies they represent, is a cross-section of industrial photography in the United States. Industrial photography has traditionally meant photography (still, motion picture, television) produced by photographic departments of corporations, institutions, and government facilities. The Nikon winners were heads of their departments. They are self-made people and most were responsible for starting their departments.

The concept of industrial photography is changing and has been broadened by in-house departments and by commercial and freelance photographers as well. It has been estimated that there are some 7,000 photographic departments in business and industry in the United States. That number is not likely to increase, because photography is only one of the media used by business and industry. Photography is included in corporate audiovisual or communications departments and is only one of the disciplines in the department, as is television. Some companies are now evaluating the function of the photography in their departments and letting attrition naturally reduce the size of the departments.

With turnover and a few new jobs, there will always be career opportunities in in-plant photography. Since many companies must, of necessity, keep technical achievements and manufacturing processes proprietary; they find it necessary to do photography within the company premises.

The benefits of working for a company can include medical insurance, paid vacation time and holidays, and even company-sponsored retirement programs. Most companies and institutions have a 35- or 40-hour week, with regular and predictable hours. Photographers are often asked to work overtime. Fringe benefits for in-house photographers sometimes include attendance at seminars, workshops, and conventions. Sometimes travel is part of performance of the job. Working in an unfamiliar environment can be a bit of a strain, in addition to being responsible for handling the equipment needed for the job.

In general, pay rates of industrial photographers are among the highest in the photographic industry. The trade-off, however, is sometime slower advancement than might be found in a commercial photographic business, and chances are the career path does not lead to great advancements within the company. Top photographers and department managers are sometimes salaried.

In preparing for a job as an in-house photographer, a degree from a recognized university is helpful, as is experience in technical photography and photo lab technology. "Experience in any kind of photography is also a plus," says Robert E. Mayer, former chief photographer for Bell & Howell. Mayer studied photography at Ohio University. Ross Sanddal, manager of photographic services for Hughes Tool Division, Houston, has a masters degree in photography from the University of Houston. Ross is a past president of the Professional Photographers of America and continues to help fellow photographers, worldwide, by appearing at convention programs and through his long-running column "Practical Pointers," in *The Professional Photographer* magazine.

Personal attributes of a good industrial photographer are competence, versatility, and imagination; he or she must be a self-starter and possess a willingness to perform any kind of photography.

**Scientific and Technical Photography**

According to the Society of Photographic Scientists and Engineers, "There are two directions you can take in photographic sciences. You can work in the application of photography to the needs of industry, medicine and government. Or you can carry out pure research aimed at the discovery and control of the basic elements of photography."

William G. Hyzer, an authority on scientific instrumentation, says, "Photography today has completely overrun its natural boundaries as a photochemical recording process and is penetrating deeply into the adjoining photoelectronic and photophysical disciplines."

The picture-making aspects of scientific and technical photography include high-speed photography and videography, photomacrography, photomicrography, holography, and color printing. The budget for research at Eastman Kodak Company amounts to over one million dollars per day. The Rochester Institute of Technology (RIT) claims there are more than 250 job titles in technical photography. Non-picture-making jobs include *mathematician, chemist, physicist,* and *photographic scientist; technical writer, laboratory supervisor,* and even a *technical representative* for a manufacturer of photographic materials and/or equipment. RIT offers both two-year AAS and four-year BS degrees in technical photography.

**Photogrammetry.**   An important part of scientific and technical photography is photogrammetry and remote sensing. Several colleges and universities offer programs in this subject. People who desire to become career photogrammetrists should acquire a fundamental background in physical mathematics in addition to scientific and technical subjects. A professional photogrammetrist is usually a college graduate; technicians have completed high school and have attended a technical college. For information on careers in photogrammetry, contact the American Society of Photogrammetry (ASP).

**Biomedical photography.**   A career in biomedical photography can be challenging and rewarding. Job opportunities can be found in medical schools, hospitals, and veterinary facilities. A visit to a local facility will let you see first-hand what the job is all about. Several schools offer programs that lead to either associate or bachelor's degrees in biomedical photography. Some schools offer master's-level courses in biomedical communications.

The Biological Photographic Association (BPA) sponsors workshops in biomedical photography and awards a Registered Biological Photographer (RBP) to those who successfully undergo the three-part program.

There are fewer than 400 RBPs in the U.S. Personal attributes are an interest in science, chiefly medicine or biology, and an interest in research, which takes perseverance and an analytical mind.

**Law enforcement, civil evidence, and forensic photography.** Forensic photography is "as great a challenge as the crime it helps to solve." The documentation of evidence is performed by photographers and technicians in police and sheriffs' departments, as well as in offices and laboratories of state highway patrols. The work in helping to solve a crime or investigate an accident can give one a feeling of pride and real accomplishment.

The Evidence Photographers International Council (EPIC) has developed the widely consulted "Standard for Crime Scene Photography." A specialty within this field is that of *examiner of questioned documents*. New developments in detection methods continue to help solve mysteries these examiners face.

Personal attributes important to photographers in this field include an inquiring mind, perseverance, patience, technical ability, and an interest in research and in police work.

Benjamin J. Cantor, who has specialized in civil evidence photography for five decades, has an engineering degree from Northeastern University and a J.D. from Boston College Law School. Cantor's experience as an expert witness in evidence photography led him to write "The Expert Witness," an important reference booklet for anyone who is interested in becoming a "skilled" or "expert" witness, regardless of the field.

**Teaching**

There are two different kinds of teaching in photography. Continuing education of professional photographers includes lectures and courses taught by instructors who are also active practitioners in the subjects they teach. For example, Veronica Cass runs a school in Hudson, Florida, as well as short courses around the world in the Veronica Cass Academy of Photographic Arts. Her classes are in retouching for negative and print enhancement. (She began her career as a retoucher and colorist.)

The other side of teaching in photography employs professional teachers to teach courses in photography at colleges and universities. In vocational and technical schools, there are both professional photographers and professional teachers. A teacher of photographic courses, in addition to being an accomplished photographer and having a solid background in photography, must have the attributes of a good communicator and the necessary skills and personal qualifications related to teaching.

Different school systems have their own academic requirements. If you want a career in teaching photography, investigate the school system in which you are interested to determine the requirements that a teacher must complete to be eligible for employment. You also need to be an accomplished photographer in the area you wish to teach, before you start teaching.

The Society for Photographic Education (SPE) is an organization of 1,500 teachers of photography at the secondary and college levels. The Professional Photographers of America has information on teaching.

**Working for the Government**

It is estimated that the federal government employs more than 7,000 photographers, most of them in the U.S. armed forces. The remaining jobs are in all major departments of the government, including agriculture, defense, justice, and the Veterans Administration. Information on qualifications and application forms for federal government jobs is available in all U.S. Post Offices.

All of the U.S. armed forces have good to excellent training programs. Many civilian photographers and technicians learned their craft in one of the armed forces.

State, county, and local governments also employ photographers and technicians. Many types of photography are produced, including law enforcement, publicity, and portraits. Information about these jobs is usually available from the civil service commission or employment office of the appropriate government.

**Other Opportunities**

There are many positions in photography other than being behind a camera. Two support services to consider are *processing and finishing* and *photo retailing*. Those who process their own film and make their own prints have spent many hours and expended much material in learning darkroom techniques. Hand-crafting in photography puts the stamp of individuality on your work. In making enlargements, the controls are in your hands—composition, exposure, special effects, the processing—each with many degrees of control. A skilled photographer/printer is a rare individual, indeed. Printing your own work is good training in becoming a commercial photographer. It behooves the photographer to have experience in all phases of the photographic process. Such experience will enhance the photographer's understanding of the craft.

**Custom printing.** Most professional photographers do not process their own film or make their own prints. These steps are handled by professional processing laboratories or in some cases by custom printers. A *custom printer* is an accomplished artist and technician who "finishes" the work of the photographer. He or she must be a good communicator, able to interact with the photographer in order to interpret how the photographer envisions the final print.

Pay for a custom printer can be higher than that of a photographer. Patience, perseverance, artistic ability, and stamina are important characteristics for a custom printer. Being a custom printer requires you to stand at an enlarger or processing tray, in the darkened room and still be able to concentrate on getting the best results possible. Be sure you are not allergic to working with the processing chemicals. In these days of predominantly color photography, the capability to make good black-and-white prints is rare indeed; premiums are paid for such work.

**Photofinishing.** Professional photographic processing laboratories offer film processing and printing to studios and corporate departments. There are employment opportunities at these labs for qualified *technicians* and *managers*.

Photofinishing of a different sort is available for the general public. These laboratories range in size from large-scale, high-volume factories to the so-called mini-labs (of which there are now 9,500) that provide one-hour service, from film to prints.

A career in photofinishing would be good for a person who is interested in knowing how machinery works and who enjoys working with equipment. Though the processing equipment is automated and little technical skill is needed to operate the systems, there is a need for people trained in the operation and maintenance of the equipment. Opportunities exist in studios, photographic departments, and in the companies that manufacture and sell such equipment.

Training is necessary, and several training schools have courses in photofinishing. Some programs lead to a two-year diploma or certificate; some lead to a four-year degree. In a typical photofinishing career path, you would start as a technician and work up to a management position or possible ownership of a processing laboratory. Part- or full-time experience in a lab will help you determine whether you wish to pursue a career in this segment of the photographic industry.

The Photo Marketing Association (PMA) has literature on careers in photofinishing, and the Association of Professional Color Labs (APCL) has employment information.

**Photo retailing.** Photo retailing is a multi-billion dollar business. Discount outlets offer equipment in the carton, off the shelf, with no follow-up after the sale; camera stores and department store camera departments have salespeople who consult with the consumer and help them decide which equipment to buy. A successful *salesperson* is knowledgeable about photography and can intelligently discuss the equipment and software and their capabilities.

The *professional dealer* is thoroughly familiar with the equipment on display—much of it complex and most of it expensive—and provides follow-up after the sale. The customer, the advanced amateur, and the professional photographer, expect a professional dealer to know the equipment and supplies; there the salesperson is truly a consultant to the photographer and is available for consultation on a daily basis.

A career in photo retailing can provide a good life. It requires not only an interest in photography but also technical training. To succeed in photo retailing, you should be at ease with the public and have a sales-oriented personality.

The Photo Marketing Association conducts courses in retailing, and a correspondence course is available on the subject from National Camera Inc.

**Photo equipment technology.** A career can be devoted to knowing what makes a camera and flash work and being able to repair and maintain the equipment in working order. Manufacturers, distributors, and dealers of photographic and audiovisual equipment depend on technicians and service companies for the maintenance and repair of the equipment. Independent repair shops and factory service departments employ full- and part-time *equipment technicians.*

Look through the pages of *Popular Photography* magazine, and you will see test reports that actually take a camera apart and analyze the parts. Reading a few of these reports will give you an idea of the complexity of these instruments. They combine mechanics and electronics that help determine exposure, control the flash, trip the shutter, and advance the film and rewind it back into the cassette. If you have an interest in what makes things work and are agile at handling small parts, if you have a knowledge of electronic controls, if you have a knack for fixing things, then a career in photo equipment technology may be for you. Facility to quickly diagnose problems and make repairs will be to your advantage, as will the ability to be innovative in modifying existing equipment for a special purpose.

Training is necessary in order to enter this field. Several schools, located primarily in the western U.S., offer courses in camera repair. Occasionally, a repair facility will have an opening to train an apprentice. National Camera Inc. offers home study courses in camera repair. For information on courses and job opportunities, contact the Society of Photo-Technologists or the Association of Audio-Visual Technicians.

Some of the job titles in photo equipment technology are *camera service specialist, inspector, modification designer, photoinstrumentation specialist, quality control technician, repair technician, test operator,* and *service manager.*

**Opportunities for Physically Handicapped**

The photographic industry has positions for physically handicapped people. If you have good use of your hands and eyes, several specialties are open to you. There are also opportunities for the deaf and for the partially sighted. Opportunities for differently-able people are particularly good in photo equipment technology, negative and transparency retouching, airbrushing, and oil coloring.

## SOME SPECIALTIES AND JOB TITLES

assistant camera operator
archivist
audiovisual equipment technician
audiovisual slide copier
audiovisual programmer
camera repairer
chief photographer
cinematographer
colorist
color production manager
commercial photographer
custom printer (black-and-white)
custom printer (color)
darkroom supervisor
darkroom technician
director of AV communications
director of photo services
director of photography
editor on photo magazine
evidence photographer
film archivist
forensic photographer
framer and matter
freelance photographer
gallery director
home economist
illustrator
industrial photographer
image analyst
image interpreter
instructor
laboratory assistant
laboratory technician
manager of photographic
   equipment
manager of photographic services
manufacturers representative
marketing specialist
media specialist
medical photographer

motion picture camera operator
museum curator
equipment technician
photofinisher
photogrammetrist
photographer
photographer's assistant
photographic artist (colorist)
photo lab technician
photography director
photographer's agent
photographer's representative
photographic processing and
   finishing manager
photographic technician
photographic technologist
photography director
photointerpreter
photo librarian
picture editor
picture researcher
public relations specialist
quality control technician
quality controller
research photographer
retail salesperson
retoucher
sales manager
senior photographer
staff photographer
still photographer
studio manager
studio receptionist
stylist
supervisor of photo electronics
supervisor of photo services
teacher
technical representative
technical writer
writer

## EDUCATION AND EXPERIENCE

You can learn the basics of photography in a relatively short time, but the most important aspect of preparing for a career in photography is preparing for the life of a photographer. Since most photographers deal in a great variety of subjects and are in contact with a varied lot, a person with a well-rounded academic education—plus life experience in the real world—stands a better chance of success than one who is not so fortunate. Take courses in the liberal arts, in sociology (including anthropology), in the arts, and in business; business should be high on your list.

Show me two people who are about to go into business as photographers—of equal artistic talent and ability—and I'll place my bet on the one who has more business acumen and happens to be the more aggressive of the two. This is a fact of life. Getting into photography is easy; staying there and progressing is quite a different matter.

Just as in medicine, law, or dentistry—where former students who didn't make it in their chosen fields have a great appreciation for medicine, law, or dentistry—those who have a deep interest in photography will likewise pursue photography as a hobby. Some even jump ahead of the photographers and become buyers of photography, the decision makers.

The most common route to the photography profession begins by making portraits. Picking up a camera and aiming it at a member of the family, a neighbor, or a friend is an easy thing to do. (An easier step in the photographic process is having the film processed and prints made by a lab.) And, every one, it seems, wants to see those pictures.

The next step is to respond to requests for prints. As the demand for your work increases (by now you will have photographed a wedding or other social event and possibly a store window), your interest in learning more about photography increases.

Reading photography magazines and books, visiting with professional photographers, joining photography organizations—camera club, local chapter of a professional organization—will lead you to a decision as to whether to go into business for yourself full-time or to seek employment as a photographer. At this point, seek further counsel. Ask, ask, ask those who are in the industry—photographers, studio owners, photo or AV department heads, photo lab managers, technicians. Listen to them.

There will come a time when you will have asked too many people for opinions and advice, and you will have to make your decision. If another profession or business would give you more enjoyment while working, choose that one, and photography can become your hobby.

The important thing is to give serious and adequate thought to and research on the subject. Ask yourself whether you have the necessary skills and training—and the perseverance—to make sufficient progress. Should you decide to study photography formally, choose your school carefully. There are a few schools that specialize in photography and several technical and art schools that offer courses in photography. Many colleges and universities offer very good courses in photography.

Once you have decided to pursue a career in photography, choose the locale in which you would like to work. Start with a major league baseball city as your center of activity. Go to the area of your choice and find the names of the photography studios and the firms with photographic or audiovisual departments.

When you know something about the community, consult the local business telephone directory and similar information that is available from the chamber of commerce or department of development. Get names and addresses of likely contacts. Get a few copies of all of the local or regional newspapers, check out the classified ads, read the business and financial pages (the Sunday paper should have such a section); find out about the business and advertising activity in the area.

Talk with studio owners and corporate audiovisual department managers. Ask about the perceived opportunities for employment or for a possible business in the area. Should you pursue commercial–illustration photography, also interview art directors at advertising agencies; get their views of the current advertising scene, even the future as they see it, as far as this type of photography in the area is concerned.

If you are interested in possible employment as an industrial or newspaper photographer, do your homework: know where the jobs are likely to be. Set up appointments with department heads and/or with personnel departments of the enterprises you would like to work for. If you or a friend or relative know someone in a company in which you are interested, ask their help in getting in touch with someone who could possibly be of assistance.

By this time, you will have surely prepared your résumé. Write individual letters to those people you wish to contact and send them a copy of your résumé. In your letter, offer to send or bring samples of your work. It is not advisable to send photographs and clippings of your work, unless there is a prior agreement for you to do so. Then, follow-up with at least one telephone call to each person—first, see if they have received your letter and résumé; then, let them know you are really interested in working for them.

**Your Portfolio**

Your portfolio must be an honest record of your own capabilities, not "typical student" work, although class exercises will show what you are capable of doing. In any event, the person conducting the interview will recognize work that was done under an instructor. Be honest and straightforward when presenting samples of your photography. Published pieces (tearsheets and clippings) are always good to have. Know the company to which you are applying and tailor your portfolio for that studio, photo department, or agency.

Your portfolio, or "book," shouldn't be elaborate. A zippered, artist's portfolio with a handle and at least one inside pocket for items too small to mount is suggested. You can slip extra sleeves of transparencies and clippings into the pocket. Put your transparencies in pocketed plastic sheets; your favorite/best transparencies, regardless of size, should be individually mounted on standard masked black cardboard mounts. Prints should be placed between clear plastic spiralbound sheets. Organize your work into series or themes. Tailor your portfolio specifically for each interview; edit your samples by rearranging, eliminating, or adding pieces, according to what you think each interviewer may want to see.

Advertise your availability—sell yourself—through classified ads in the local newspapers and through professional and trade periodicals. You will need at least two months' time to get responses to such an ad in a magazine. You might also consider registering with a personnel agency.

When you are selecting a locale, you are well advised to stay away from major metropolitan areas such as New York, Chicago, or Los Angeles—unless you know that you have unusual talent, plus the ability to compete for a job in such an area, and you can afford to live there for quite a while while you are looking for a job.

If you are a member in good standing, ask your professional photographer society for guidance. Consult the career counselor at your school, and/or work through your school's placement service in pursuing employment. Be aware, however, that photography is not like other disciplines—such as business, engineering, or science—the recruiters aren't looking for you. You have to be the agressor.

## Continuing Education

It is an accepted fact of life in photography that it is necessary to continue one's vocational enhancement. Techniques in photography are forever changing, and equipment is always undergoing improvements to help the photographer do a better job. The marketing of photography, particularly if you are an independent freelancer or a studio owner, is getting increasingly important. Sophisticated marketing strategies have been developed by companies like Creative Access, which conducts "The Self-Promotion Workshops" for the creative professional in major cities throughout the country. Continuing education not only helps the photographer keep up with current developments and changes, it helps in personal and company growth, providing practical, proven ideas for improving technique and business.

Associations and societies, as well as not-for-profit institutions, sponsor conventions, seminars, short courses, and workshops devoted to every aspect of the photography business. This continuing education is available at reasonable cost, and sessions are held at convenient locations for a minimum of time. There are also privately-run workshops and industry-sponsored short courses.

The pioneer—and premier—group in continuing education is the 105-year-old Professional Photographers of America which sponsors conventions, seminars, workshops, and the Winona International School of Professional Photography, founded in 1921. The Winona facilities are located in a Chicago suburb and are open year round. Three- and five-day training and refresher courses cover specialized techniques that most working photographers use frequently. Hands-on training is provided by instructors actively engaged in their specialties. Each course offered at Winona has its "learning level," courses in many specialty areas are offered in basic, entry, intermediate, advanced, and specialized levels. Prerequisites are stated for each course and "sequential learning opportunities" are offered.

The student seeking a career in photography should get involved in a professional group as early as possible. Membership is useful in making contacts and in becoming part of a network, which could be the beginning of a life-long association. Belonging to a professional group is a two-way street: you gain by learning from others; you also gain by sharing with others as you grow.

*A Survey, College Instruction in Photography, Motion Picture/ Graphic Arts/Still Photography* (Publications T-17) contains a listing of the majority of schools that offer courses in photography. It is available at libraries or can be ordered from Eastman Kodak Company, 343 State St., Rochester, NY 14650.

A selected list of schools appears in *Opportunities in Photography Careers* by Bervin Johnson, Robert E. Mayer, and Fred Schmidt (VGM Career Horizons, 1991).

## CONTINUING EDUCATION FOR PROFESSIONAL PHOTOGRAPHERS

The following selected facilities and groups accept registrations from beginners and entry-level applicants.

Most associations and societies conduct lectures and short courses during their conventions. See the Associations and Societies listing for names and addresses.

Ansel Adams Gallery
P.O. Box 455
Yosemite National Park, CA
  95389

Short courses in using the view camera.

American Society of Magazine
  Photographers
419 Park Avenue, Suite 1407
New York, NY 10016

Lectures and short courses for freelancers.

Brooks Institute
801 Alston Rd.
Santa Barbara, CA 93108

Three-day courses on a variety of subjects.

| | |
|---|---|
| Creative Access<br>415 West Superior<br>Chicago, IL 60610 | Traveling short courses on marketing. |
| Dynamic Graphics Educational Foundation<br>6000 North Forest Park Dr.<br>P.O. Box 1901<br>Peoria, IL 61656 | Five-day courses on audiovisual techniques. |
| Law Enforcement Security Markets<br>Eastman Kodak Company<br>5th Fl., Bldg 20<br>Rochester, NY 14650 | Courses and seminars in law enforcement and forensic photography. |
| Maine Photographic Workshops<br>Rockport, ME 04856 | 14 weeks of summer courses. |
| National Camera Inc.<br>Technical Training Division<br>Denver, CO 80210 | Home study courses in camera repair and photo retail sales. |
| Parsons School of Design, Photo Dept.<br>The New School<br>66 Fifth Ave.<br>New York, NY 10011 | Focus Workshop Series, one-week symposia. |
| Photo Marketing Association International<br>3000 Picture Pl.<br>Jackson, MI 49201 | Short courses in photo retailing. |
| Rochester Institute of Technology<br>T & E Seminar Center<br>One Lomb Memorial Dr.<br>P.O. Box 9887<br>Rochester, NY 14623 | RIT Photograpy Workshops. |
| University of Wisconsin-Extension<br>929 North Sixth St.<br>Milwaukee, WI 53203 | High-Speed Motion Analysis Systems & Techniques, one-week seminar. |
| Veronica Cass Academy of Photographic Arts<br>P.O. Box 5519<br>Hudson, FL 33567 | Residence courses and traveling workshops in retouching, oil coloring, and airbrushing. |

Wedding Photographers
International (WPI)
P.O. Box 2003, 1312 Lincoln Blvd.
Santa Monica, CA 90406

Traveling short courses in bridal
and wedding photography.

Winona International School of
Professional Photography
350 North Wolf Rd.
Mt. Prospect, IL 60056

Three- and five-day residential
courses in all aspects.

## SOURCES OF INFORMATION

**Associations and
Societies**

Addresses for these organizations appear in Appendix A at the back of
this book.

Advertising Photographers of America (APA)
American Society of Magazine Photographers (ASMP)
American Society of Photogrammetry (ASP)
American Society of Picture Professionals (ASPP)
Association Audio-Visual Technicians (AAVT)
Association for Multi-Image International (AMI)
Association of Professional Color Laboratories (APCL)
Biological Photographers Association (BPA)
Evidence Photographers International Council (EPIC)
National Association of Photographic Equipment Technicians (NAPET)
National Press Photographers Association (NPPA)
Photo Marketing Association International (PMA)
Professional Photographers of America (PP of A)
Society for Photographic Education (SPE)
Society of Photographic Scientists and Engineers (SPSE)
Society of Photo-Technologists (SPT)
Wedding Photographers International (WPI)

## PERIODICALS

Addresses for these periodical publications appear in Appendix B at the
back of this book.

*Advanced Imaging*
*American Photographer*
*Aperture*
*Computer Pictures*
*Darkroom & Creative Camera
  Techniques*
*Darkroom Photography*
*Functional Photography*
*FYI, For Your Information*

*Industrial Photography*
*Lens' On Campus*
*News Photographer*
*Photo District News*
*Peterson's PhotoGraphic*
*Photo/Design*
*Photographic Science and
  Engineering*
*Photographic/Video Trade News*

*Photo Electronic Imaging*           *Photogrammetric Engineering and*
*Photo Lab Management*                   *Remote Sensing*
*Photo Marketing*                    *The Professional Photographer*
*Photo Weekly*                       *The Rangefinder*
*Popular Photography*                *Studio Photography*


## RECOMMENDED READING

Bailey, Adrian. *Illustrated Dictionary of Photography.* New York: Simon
    & Schuster, 1988.
Edgerton, Harold E. and James R. Killian, Jr. *Moments of Vision.* Cam-
    bridge, MA: MIT Press, 1979.
Faber, John. *Great News Photos.* New York: Dover Publications, Inc.,
    1978.
Johnson, Bervin, Robert E. Mayer, and Fred Schmidt. *Opportunities in
    Photography Careers.* Lincolnwood, IL: VGM Career Horizons, 1991.
O'Connor, Michael. *Image Bank.* New York: Amphoto, 1985.
Perweiller, Gary. *Secrets of Studio Still Life Photography.* New York:
    Amphoto, 1984.

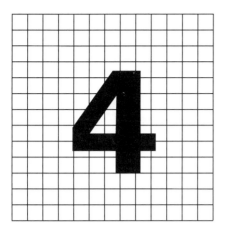

# FILM

There is more professional and academic concern for the future of cinema in the United States today than ever before. There is a greater variety and number of opportunities of work in the field, especially as film is recognized as an interdisciplinary medium, and as the state of the art is advanced through the efforts of talented, disciplined, and knowledgeable film artists, teachers, and students.

Robert W. Wagner, *Guide to College Courses in Film and Television,* The American Film Institute, Washington, D.C.

Film probably provides the broadest and most varied creative opportunities of the mass media. After being a scientific curiosity during its earliest two decades, it has developed into a universal art form that transcends cultural differences. It is the most international medium, as it developed into a language in itself in the days of silent movies. The advent of sound enhanced the film language, making it a more complete communication medium.

In its early days, this scientific curiosity was used to document news and the phenomena of the universe. Later, entertainment became the prime function of the medium. Business-minded people turned it into an industry, while purists who esteemed its creative potential continued to experiment with the art form. To this day, entertainment still dominates the film world, although the documentation of reality and knowledge continues to be a major function of the medium.

Movies today can be divided into the broad categories of feature, documentary, educational, industry, and governmental films. Commercials could be added as another category, although they are mostly produced for advertising and publicity purposes.

The film industry in the United States has gone through tremendous changes since the advent of television. For years, it has been identified with the name *Hollywood*. The major studios dominated the production and distribution of feature films (which had a large domestic and overseas market). Several major studios are less involved in production; instead, they do financing and distribution. Production companies are set up for individual films. Six big studios—Columbia Pictures, MGM/United Artists, Warner Brothers, Twentieth Century Fox, Paramount, and Universal—dominate the scene. There are also a few medium sized studios and a growing number of independent production companies.

A few years ago, independents were associated with low-budget films. That is not necessarily the case any more. Some independent productions, like *Indiana Jones: The Temple of Doom,* are now big-budget ventures. Miniaturization of equipment has made location shooting easier for independent filmmakers, letting them shoot on natural locations instead of expensive sound stages. However, in spite of the increase in the number of independent films, the feature film industry is still dominated by studio conglomerates, which account for 75 percent of the feature films produced in the U.S.

Television has become both the worst adversary and the biggest benefactor of the film industry. It has changed the role of film from a primary art and entertainment form to the primary source of another medium. Today, 50 percent of the prime-time programming of the networks and 80 percent of the programming of independent stations are produced on film. Only one third of feature films are now made for theatrical release; the rest are packaged for television.

Motion picture producers used to collect 50 percent of the box office revenues from the distributors. Television channels, especially the cable movie channels, pay only a fraction of that for telecast rights of movies that are not released in theaters. The reduction in income has affected the movie industry. The movies without theatrical release also reduce jobs in distribution and exhibition, which were at one time a major source of revenue for the motion picture industry.

The introduction of home video cassette recorders (VCRs) created a new outlet for movies. In spite of piracy, the industry has been able to make substantial gains through this new outlet.

The 18,000-plus movie theaters across the U.S. continue to provide the foundation for the industry. In 1984, the industry employed over 109,000 persons, according to U.S. Bureau of Labor statistics. The annual box office gross more than doubled in a decade, $3.7 billion in 1983 compared to $1.6 billion in 1973. The main reason for that increase is the increase in ticket prices in recent years. Today, more than 75 percent of the moviegoers in the U.S. are under 30 years of age; they have been enabling the industry to outlive the challenges of television and video and enjoy reasonable growth.

## WHERE THE JOBS ARE

The jobs in the motion picture industry are in production, distribution, and exhibition. However, persons interested in careers in film usually explore mostly the production area which deals with the making of motion pictures. The production of feature films for entertainment is the most popular pursuit in filmmaking. However, documentary films, educational films, industrial films, and government films are also important to the industry. Unfortunately, many beginners are reluctant to seek a position in these types of filmmaking which could bring them valuable experience and provide them a stepping stone to the feature film industry.

According to U.S. Department of Labor statistics, 220,000 persons were employed in the motion picture industry in 1984. Out of these, 189,000 are involved in production work. However, a large number were not employed on a full-time basis. Fewer than 80,000 persons are on established payrolls of the industry.

Most jobs in the film industry are done on a freelance, part-time, or contractual basis. Consequently, it is hard to see a ladder of upward mobility as you can in other communications professions.

**Feature Films**

The United States produces approximately 200 feature films a year. The year 1982 showed the lowest number since 1976, with a total of only 184. Out of these, 105 were made overseas. Of the foreign starts, 35 were by major studios and 70 by independent producers. Although the number of domestic productions increased in 1983, producers tend to make films abroad to cash in on lower labor costs and high foreign exchange rates. This trend has reduced the number of domestic jobs in the motion picture industry.

The entertainment feature film industry is concentrated in Los Angeles and New York. People who want to pursue film careers in this part of the industry must generally relocate to these cities, although other major cities are trying to attract independent producers by providing tax incentives and better production facilities.

**Documentaries**

The documentary film industry keeps growing, thanks to the advances of technology. The introduction of the 16mm and super-8mm formats made the task of the documentary filmmakers easy. Miniature equipment in the 35mm format has also contributed to the ease of production. The moderate cost of renting the equipment prompted many individuals to undertake documentary production. Public television, commercial television stations, and cable television provide a market for their products.

Many people who want to get into the feature film industry start with documentary filmmaking. Some production companies specialize in documentary filmmaking and are happy hunting grounds for beginners.

**Educational Films**

In recent years, educational films (especially films in the 16mm format) have had a steadily growing market. About 1,700 educational films are produced every year. Major book publishers and producers of educational materials have been involved in the production of educational films.

**Industrial Films**

The audiovisual departments of organizations of the corporate and non-profit sector are involved in in-house movie production. Over 9,000 such films are produced annually. Sometimes, the projects are assigned to outside production companies. These films are mostly used as public relations tools and information sources for employees, stockholders, and consumers. They are also extensively used for training programs.

**Government Films**

Each year, the different agencies of the federal and state governments produce many training and propaganda films. The annual output of such films is close to 2,000 in recent years. Some of the films are made using in-house production facilities and others are assigned to independent filmmakers. Employment opportunities in the film departments of government agencies are rather easily available for newcomers; they are ideal training grounds for new talent.

**Commercials**

Commercials are usually made for the clients of advertising agencies whose main medium is television. Major advertising agencies have extensive production facilities. Most advertising agencies contract with independent production companies to produce commercials, although some agencies do have in-house production capability. The commercials provide as much challenge as other kinds of film and demand good technical skills and creativity.

### THE JOBS

The best way of identifying the jobs available in the film industry is to lean back in a movie theater seat as most patrons walk out and read the seemingly never-ending list of credits at the end. Hundreds of them, big and small, roll down the screen, challenging the eye. Add to them the credits in the beginning of the movie and that will provide a complete list of jobs and on-screen roles involved in the making of that moving picture. While a major feature film will contain hundreds of credits, a short film or documentary carries just a few. The jobs in filmmaking mostly pertain to writing, production, direction, cinematography, lighting, sound recording, and editing.

**Scriptwriting**

Movies begin with a concept or an idea which is developed into a script. The concept may be a figment of a writer's or filmmaker's imagination or a slice from real life. In either case, the *scriptwriter* develops the concept into a script. Scriptwriters work through *agents* who handle their contracts. Sometimes the original idea may come from the director, and the writer is asked to develop it, or an existing literary work may be adapted into a screenplay by a scriptwriter.

An original idea may be developed by the writer who submits it to filmmakers in the form of a *treatment*. Once the treatment is approved, the *screenplay* is prepared. The last stage is the *shooting script;* it contains the technical details and guidelines on shots, camera angles, and lighting. In many films, the shooting script stage is handled by the director, and the duty of the scriptwriter ends with the screenplay.

Scriptwriters work closely with directors, who are responsible for translating words into pictures. Often alterations are made in the script according to the requests or demands of the director.

**Production**

**Producer.**   The *producer* is the person responsible for the financial aspects of the film. When a major studio is providing the finances, a producer is hired to head the production company set up for the production of that film. In independent filmmaking, the financial responsibility falls on the person who ventures to make the film. Usually, the independent producer obtains backing from distributors who advance sizeable amounts of money at different stages of production.

Although he or she is mainly responsible for the business side of the movie, the producer works closely with the director, particularly on the choice of the script and the leading actors. These decisions have a major impact on the ultimate financial prospects and success of the film.

**Production manager.**   The producer works with the *production manager* who works out the detailed budget and prepares the production schedule. The production manager is in charge of the actual production. He or she oversees the entire production process from the planning stage to the editing stage. Major decisions such as locations, budgets, and schedules of cast and crew are assigned to the production manager. He or she prepares the budget breakdown and puts together the shooting schedule. Search for locations, negotiations, and releases are her or his responsibilities. Housing and transportation of the cast and crew is another major responsibility of the production manager. Finally, he or she keeps an eye on each day's production, makes sure that the project is moving on schedule, and prepares daily reports on its progress.

**Direction**

Direction is the essence of filmmaking and that is why the director is also called the *filmmaker.* In full-length feature films, the task of direction cannot be handled by one person alone, so assistant directors are hired. Their numbers vary according to the size and complexity of the shoot.

**Director.**   The task of translating the written word to visual images accompanied by an appropriate soundtrack belongs to the director. He or she is the artist who creates the movie, guiding the work of hundreds of people from the scriptwriter to the editor. He or she is in charge of the artistic and technical aspects of the film. The responsibility for the final product rests on the director.

The director makes most of the major decisions regarding the making of a movie. He or she approves the selection of the cast as well as the technical crew and has the final say on the costumes, sets, and location. Many directors closely supervise photography and editing; they decide how each scene should be shot. They are in charge of the rehearsals and guide the actors. Many directors prefer to write the shooting script from the screenplay provided by a scriptwriter. Some also edit the film. In short, the director supervises the work of the entire cast and crew during shooting.

**Unit production manager.**   The *unit production manager* is the person in charge of production units on location. He or she is entrusted the task of searching for and surveying potential locations and of working out the specific requirements of shooting there. He or she is usually helped by the assistant directors.

**First assistant director.**   The actual execution of many of the tasks of the director is delegated to the *first assistant director.* He or she is in charge of organizing the production process. The shooting schedule is usually her or his responsibility. He or she makes sure that call sheets are given to the cast and crew in advance. During the shooting, the first assistant director assists the director and keeps a close watch over the cast and crew.

Often, the director leaves the details of the production to the first assistant and her or his helpers. Crowd control is one of the major tasks of the assistant director. Occasionally he or she directs some of the routine scenes of the movie and background action.

**Second assistant director.**   The person (or persons) who assists the first assistant director is the *second assistant director.* The main responsibilities of the second assistant are distribution of callsheets, handling of extras, transportation of equipment and crew to locations, arrangement for food and accommodations for the cast and crew, as well as the coordination of the production staff.

**Continuity person (script supervisor).**   In the past, the person performing this task was called the *scriptgirl.* The *continuity person* is the eyes and ears of the director. He or she keeps track of the production and takes notes to assure continuity of time breakdown. Careful notes of the span of days, months, or years between sequences have to be maintained. Breakdown of all props and makeup in different scenes has to be recorded. Chronology has to be accurately monitored as the filming is not done according to the natural sequence of events. Negligence on the part of this person results in illogical discrepancies of time, costumes, makeup, and other details in different scenes.

## Art Direction

The art direction department handles the physical environment of the film that determines mood and atmosphere. The preparation of sets and props, the designing of wardrobe, hairstyling, makeup, and the creation of some special effects come under this department.

**Art director.** The *art director* supervises the above-mentioned operations and is responsible for the physical look of the film. He or she takes charge of the production of sketches of set designs and miniatures, and selects the locations in consultation with the director.

The art director is in charge of the construction of the set. A small army of carpenters, painters, laborers, electricians, and technicians work under her or his supervision. The art director is assisted by *chargeman scenic artist* and *journeyman scenic artist*.

**Scenic artists.** The chargeman scenic artist prepares the miniature models and the journeyman scenic artist assists. They also take care of plastering and painting the sets and doing other decorative work on the walls of the sets.

**Shop person.** The shop person is in charge of all tools and materials required by the artists. He or she supplies materials and supervises the cleaning operation after the work is done.

## Cinematography

The task of capturing the scene on film is called cinematography. The *cinematographer,* formerly called cameraman or film *photographer,* and her or his assistants works with the cameras and lights to film whatever the director wants on celluloid. Often several takes of the scene are required; demanding directors with budgets to back them may ask for a dozen or more takes.

**Cinematographer.** The cinematographer is also called the *director of photography*. He or she is responsible for the visual aspect and thereby the mood of the movie. He or she works very closely with the director.

The cinematographer does not operate the camera, although he or she checks the framing through the viewfinder. He or she works in conjunction with the lab to assure the quality of processing and printing.

The cinematographer determines the photographic style of the film, in consultation with the director. He or she also makes the decisions on lighting and camera positions. The selection of different types of shots and the lenses required for them is one of the cinematographer's major tasks. In short, he or she composes the shots of the movie.

**Camera operator.**   The cinematographer is assisted in the composition of shots by the *camera operator* who works with the *first assistant camera operator* (also known as the *focus puller*). The operator handles all camera movements and is responsible for the focus of the shots. Smooth camera movements are important for good photography.

**First assistant camera operator.**   The main charge of the first assistant camera operator is the maintenance of camera. He or she checks the equipment at preproduction time and prepares and loads the camera for shooting. He or she is responsible for the change of lenses and filters during shooting. He or she has to make sure the camera is running at the right film speed and is on focus after each shot. He or she also helps with the crew call sheet.

**Second assistant camera operator.**   The second assistant helps the first assistant in these tasks. He or she operates the slate and clapsticks before the takes and takes care of the actors' marks. This job also involves considerable paperwork, as the second assistant is in charge of the inventory of the equipment and has to keep records of camera rentals and repairs. The second assistant also handles the shipping of the stock to the lab and keeps the lab report on the dailies.

**Key grip.**   The *key grip* determines the placement of cameras and their movements as required by the camera operator. The key grip also places the order for equipment and works with assistants who take care of a variety of things such as the placement of reflection materials and hanging of gels.

**Gaffer.**   The charge of lighting belongs to the *gaffer*. The gaffer helps the cinematographer with creative suggestions on lighting and later sets up different kinds of lighting during the filming.

**Sound Recording**

The staff of the sound recording department records dialogues and sounds during the filming. The *sound recording engineer* (or mixer) supervises this operation.

**Sound engineer.**   All live sound generated during the production is recorded under the supervision of the sound engineer or mixer. The entire dialogue of the actors and other sounds are recorded during the shooting. The sound engineer is responsible for the selection of microphones and determines the level of sound during the recording to assure quality of reproduction.

**Recordist.**   The *recordist* runs individual tape recorders and assists the sound engineer in setting up the equipment.

**Boom operator.**   The setting up of the microphones and the operation of the boom is the responsibility of the *boom operator*. He or she must make sure that the microphones do not appear in the film frame during the shooting.

## Editing

Editing is one of the parts of filmmaking least visible to the public. However, it is perhaps the most critical stage of the making of a film. Many a bad movie has been saved on the editing table by creative and talented editors who have given new meanings and dynamism to the strips of film submitted to them. Similarly, a well-shot film can be ruined by unimaginative editors; for this very reason, most of the masters of world cinema prefer to edit their own films. They believe that good cinema is made on the editing table.

**Editor.**   The dailies (the film shot every day) is processed in the lab and then sent to the *editor* for the 'rough cut.' The editor looks at the footage, selects the best shots, and assembles them in the most effective sequence. The rough cut is viewed by the director and the cinematographer on a daily basis during the production itself. At the postproduction stage, sound and film are synchronized, and an answer print is made.

The editor assures dramatic continuity for the film and determines its pace and tempo. He or she determines the final combination of sight and sound as it appears on the screen and assures the organic unity and aesthetic beauty of the film as a whole. Until the editing is complete, the film is in disconnected bits and pieces.

**Dubbing editor.**   The *dubbing editor* is the main helper of the editor at the postproduction or rerecording stage. He or she selects the sound tracks and music tracks for mixing and adds special sound effects to the dialogue and natural sound tracks.

**Assistant editor.**   The *assistant editor* is in charge of preparing the editing rooms by reserving them and setting them up. He or she also works on the synchronization of the dailies and breaking down the dailies.

**Editing room assistant.**   The rather boring routines of editing are the task of the *editing room assistant*. These duties include splicing, patching, and rewinding of film. Coding and storing of the film are also assigned to the editing room assistant. These are also the basic lessons for any beginner who wants to learn the art of editing.

## Other Jobs

A variety of other jobs exist in the film industry, and a few of them warrant special attention here.

**Actors.**   Stardom is associated with acting, but not all of the roles in a motion picture are the glamorous ones featuring leading stars. Leading actors and actresses do exert substantial influence on the makeup of many movies. However, the majority of actors are often unemployed or without the kind of roles they would most like to play. For them, it is long hours and hard work for small roles.

The creative or artistic satisfaction of performing for an audience is missing in movie acting, since the whole film is not rehearsed or filmed in sequence. Often, little of the original footage appears in the final cut, adding to the frustration of the performers.

**Musicians.**  Musicians in the film industry belong to two categories: the *music directors* and *composers* who are responsible for the score and the *musicians* who play instruments for the rendition of the score. Some of the scores are original creations; others are adaptations of existing material.

**Makeup artists.**  The work of the makeup artist and her or his assistants consists of preparing and applying the makeup to the actors. Often it is a monotonous routine, but some unusual roles call for originality and creativity in the makeup artist.

## EDUCATION AND EXPERIENCE

The film industry is one of the most demanding career choices for beginners. The beginnings are hard for most aspirants. They have to start at the very bottom and prove themselves before getting a major assignment. A tremendous amount of patience and perseverance is required of them. Besides artistic and technical skills, they should possess considerable organizational ability, as the profession requires rigorous planning and scheduling of time and efficient budgeting of finances. The ability to work under deadline pressures is a must for the members of this industry. The ability to work with others and the willingness to take direction—in fact, to take orders—are essential. One should also be flexible enough to make adjustments and accommodations.

Scriptwriters need writing skills and creativity. In addition, they must also master the elements of the film language and the basics of filmmaking; that mastery will enable them to write for the visual medium of film.

Producers and production staff should possess business and organizational skills, as they handle money and people. Diplomatic skills will be important in dealing with agents, cast, and crew. The skills of negotiation and problem solving will be added assets for them.

Directors should be versatile people with sound knowledge of the different aspects of filmmaking, ranging from scriptwriting to editing. They should also have the knack and patience for working with the different kinds of people who collaborate in the making of a movie.

Cinematographers must have formal training in their craft, either at a college or institute or through apprenticeship in the industry. They also must have the ability to work with and take orders from the director, even when they may not agree with her or his ideas. Editors need formal education or extensive apprenticeship experience to be eligible for their trade; they must be able to understand the mind of the director and collaborate with her or him in bringing the film to proper completion.

Actors need talent and discipline. Most have to struggle for years to get a major role; in the meantime, they have survived through odd jobs. Even after the first role is obtained, there is no guarantee of success or steady employment. Perseverance is the name of the game. Initially, talent alone is not sufficient; formal training from a university or acting institute is required. Basic skills of dancing and singing are very useful for the beginner.

According to the American Film Institute *Guide to College Courses in Film and Television,* 1,607 colleges and universities in the United States offer courses in film and television; 146 schools offer degrees in film; 45 offer masters' degrees, and 11 have doctoral programs. One third of the schools offer production courses. A complete listing of these institutions are listed in *Peterson's Guide* (P.O. Box 2123 Princeton, NJ 08540).

The Borough of Manhattan Community College (BMCC) is funded by the New York State Education Department, to provide instruction in videotape editing to persons already skilled in film production techniques. This tuition-free retraining program is offered to bonafide members of participating unions. Classes are limited to 16 students, per each of five ten-week sessions. For information, contact Borough of Manhattan Community College, 199 Chambers Street, New York, NY 10007.

**Private Institute Training**

In addition to colleges and universities, a number of private institutes (most located in New York and Los Angeles) offer training in the various aspects of filmmaking, such as scriptwriting, direction, editing, and acting.

The Directors Guild of America offers a training program for six or seven students a year; those who complete the training are eligible for the job of second assistant director.

The Academy of Motion Picture Arts and Sciences offers an internship program through the American Film Institute for six or seven prospective directors, each of whom work on a feature film as intern for a small stipend.

The American Film Institute offers a one-year program through its Center for Advanced Film Studies; 80–85 students are admitted to different specialty areas in directing, production, cinematography, screenwriting, and production design.

A list of other apprenticeship and training programs is provided at the end of the chapter.

**Experience**

Experience is the main credential for a job in filmmaking. Students of colleges and universities should build up their portfolios with their scripts and student films. Internship with a film production company during college is an invaluable experience.

Participation in film festivals is another stepping stone for aspiring filmmakers. Several competitions and festivals are held nationally to locate budding talent. Student films are well received at these events. Awards from these competitions enhance the credentials of filmmakers. (A list of these competitions can be found in the AFI *Guide to College Courses in Film and Television.*)

In almost every area of filmmaking, newcomers have to start at the bottom. Before turning scriptwriter, aspiring writers usually acquire credit by publishing some of their writing in other media. They should also write some scripts for submission at interviews. Many attempt to write teleplays for episodes of television series or stage plays to accumulate credits. (The minimum requirement for membership in the Writer's Guild of America is that a person has been employed as a writer for screen, television, radio, or that he or she has sold original material to the media. The Guild does not find employment for its members.)

The job of producer comes after a long wait and years of experience, first as production assistant and then as production manager.

The road to the director's chair is also long and narrow. Often one has to start as a continuity person and then move on to the position of second assistant director. Even the internship program of the Director's Guild of America Arts and Sciences is not for training directors, but second assistant directors. The next move is to the position of first assistant director and then unit production manager. There is no automatic promotion to the director's chair after that. Directors come from all areas of filmmaking.

Cinematographers go through similar stages of progress. The best entry-level position possible for most newcomers is that of the second assistant cameraman. The next step is being the first assistant cameraman.

Many sound recordists started their careers as boom operators. Gradually they get into recording and end up as sound engineers. Similarly, the boring routine of an editing room assistant has been the beginning of many brilliant careers in editing.

**Apprenticeship and Training Programs**

Academy of Motion Picture Arts and
  Sciences
8949 Wilshire Blvd.
Beverly Hills, CA 90211
  Academy Internship Program

American Film Institute
  Center for Advanced Film Studies:

Directing Workshop for Women
(18-month program)
Fellowship Program in Filmmaking
(one-year program)

International Alliance of Theatrical and
    Stage Employees and Moving Picture
    Machine Operators (IATSE)
1515 Broadway, Suite 601
New York, NY 10036
    Apprenticeship Programs (2–4 years)

National Academy of Television Arts and
    Sciences
1560 Broadway, Suite 503
New York, NY 10036
    Script Development Workshop

The Directors Guild of America
116 East 27th Street
New York, NY 10016
    DGA Training Program

## UNIONS

Unions are an integral part of the motion picture industry. They control the destinies not only of their established members but also of aspirants to the film world. They determine to a great extent the employment prospects of newcomers.

Writers, actors, producers, and directors call their unions *guilds,* others call them *unions.* The former are not associated with AFL-CIO, and that probably helps them maintain their elitist image.

Two unions dominate the film industry: the International Alliance of Theatrical and Stage Employees (IATSE), with 900 locals established in 1928, and the National Association of Broadcasting Employees and Technicians (NABET), founded in the 1950s.

Theoretically, a newcomer need not be a member of the union to work in the film industry. However, without work experience, one cannot be eligible for union membership. It is a vicious circle. Most film production companies and television networks sign a union shop contract with the locals. Nonunion members can be hired for 30 working days; after that they must pay the union initiation fee and membership dues to continue working on the job. They do not have to become formal members, but they have to meet the terms of union shop contract. If they do not, the union can demand their dismissal.

While many union members are unemployed, very few organizations will take the risk of hiring nonunion members. Although the unions are big hurdles for a newcomer, they serve the interest of the workers by defining their job titles, job descriptions, duties, and remuneration.

The Directors Guild of America grants membership to anyone who has been hired as director by a movie or television production company, local station, or independent producer. At present, the Guild has more than 4,400 directors; 1,900 assistant directors and unit managers; and 1,500 associate directors, stage managers, and production assistants. The Guild maintains a qualification list of people with appropriate experience in each category and makes it available to prospective employers. It does not directly find employment for its members.

The Writers Guild of America, which has more than 2,800 members on the east coast and 6,200 members on the west coast, admits people who have written scripts for the media. Its main service to its members is the TV market list regularly published in the Writers Guild newsletter. It also allows members and nonmembers to register their scripts, so that it can provide evidence of the copyright of the author. Like the Directors Guild, it does not provide employment services.

## SOURCES OF INFORMATION

Film is an exciting medium and a unique industry. Searching for a job in this field is a challenging process. Jobs are seldom advertised. Personal contacts are often the best leads for employment. There is no way of predicting the rate of advancement; the steps are not well defined.

Individual initiative has a lot to do with advancement in this field. The glamor of the profession or a dedication to the art of film drives people to the top. This field belongs to dreamers and survivors. The world of film is a world of reality and illusion. So also is the process of making it a lifetime career.

**Associations and Societies**

Listed below are the major associations and societies in the field. Addresses appear in Appendix A.

> Actors Equity Association
> Academy of Motion Picture Arts and Sciences
> American Cinema Editors
> American Film Institute
> American Society of Cinematographers, Inc.
> Association of Independent Video and Filmmakers
> Association of Motion Picture and Television Producers
> Directors Guild of America
> National Academy of Television Arts and Sciences
> Producers Guild of America
> Society of Motion Picture and Television Engineers

Screen Actors Guild
Writers Guild of America

## PERIODICALS

If you are interested in a career in the film industry, you should keep abreast of developments through trade publications. The publications listed here will be useful for people involved in any aspect of the cinema. If you are involved in film production, you should also read video trade magazines listed in Chapter 7.

Addresses for periodical publishers appear in Appendix B.

*Amazing Cinema*
*American Cinematographer*
*American Film*
*The Big Reel*
*Boxoffice*
*Cineaste*
*Cinefantastique*
*Cinemagic*
*Film Comment*
*Film Culture*
*The Film Journal*
*Film News*
*Film Quarterly*
*Films in Review*
*Film & Video*
*The Hollywood Reporter*
*The Hollywood Studio Magazine*
*The Independent*
*Journal of the University Film and Video Association*
*Literature/Film Quarterly*
*Movie Trends*
*Quarterly Review of Film Studies*
*Variety*

## RECOMMENDED READING

*Film History*
Ellis, Jack C. *A History of Film*. 3rd ed. Englewood Cliffs, NJ: Prentice-Hall, 1990.
Knight, Arthur. *The Liveliest Art*. New York: Mentor, 1979.

Mast, Gerald. *A Short History of the Movies.* 3rd ed. New York: Bobbs-Merrill, 1981.

*Film Theories*

Dick, Bernard F. *Anatomy of Film.* New York: St. Martin's Press, 1975.

Sobchack, Thomas and Vivian C. Sobchack. *Introduction to Film.* 2nd ed. Glenview, IL: Scott Foresman, 1987.

Mast, Gerald and Marshall Cohen. *Film Theory and Criticism.* New York: Oxford University Press, 1985.

*Documentary*

Barsam, Richard M. *Nonfiction Film: A Critical History.* Indianapolis: Indiana University Press, 1992.

Jacobs, Lewis. *The Documentary Tradition.* 2nd ed. New York: W.W. Norton, 1979.

*Film Direction*

Lipton, Lenny. *Independent Filmmaking.* New York: Simon & Schuster, 1983.

Malkiewicz, J. Kris, *Cinematography.* Englewood Cliffs, NJ: Prentice-Hall, 1989.

Roberts, Kenneth H. and Win Sharples, *A Primer for Filmmaking.* New York: MacMillan, 1971.

Sherman, Eric. *Directing the Film.* Los Angeles: Acrobat Books, 1988.

*Film Careers*

Bone, Jan. *Opportunities in Film Careers.* Lincolnwood, IL: VGM Career Horizons, 1990.

Greenspon, Jaq. *Careers for Film Buffs.* Lincolnwood, IL: VGM Career Horizons, 1993.

# RADIO AND AUDIO

Radio is in many ways the most versatile, adaptable, and efficient of all media. In its ability to reach and cater to a multitude of people with instantaneous and ever-changing local service, it is unique.*

*Elmo Ellis, *Opportunities in Broadcasting Careers* (Lincolnwood, IL: VGM Career Horizons, 1992.

The thirties and forties are regarded as the golden age of radio. It was the time when, in 1937 during a newspaper strike, New York City's mayor, Fiorello La Guardia, took to the radio air waves to read aloud to children the comic strips that regularly appeared in the New York papers. When Burns and Allen, Jack Benny and Bob Hope softened the hard times of the Depression with their wit, when Frank Sinatra hosted the weekly *Hit Parade* and Jack Armstrong came to be known as the All-American Boy.

Communicating through the medium of sound alone is a challenge. Radio as a mass medium leaves the communicator with little control over the audience. Radio also has the ability to inform and entertain without visual support. Moreover, it provides an immediacy no other medium can match; radio is a vital link in times of emergency and crisis.

Orson Welles proved the "believability" of radio with his 1938 "War of the Worlds" broadcast, which caused millions of people to believe that the Martians had landed. Stan Freberg, a master of audio and innovator in radio advertising, used Jack Benny's sound effect person in his recording of "The United States of America" (USA), a fine example of radio production. Segments of USA are still played (after 20 years) occasionally on radio. Jack Benny's old radio programs are aired even today.

Garrison Keillor is at the forefront of the reemergence of radio as an entertainment medium. His "Lake Wobegon" on the weekly "Prairie Home Companion" public radio broadcasts is a mythical small town set in the heartlands of Minnesota and is yet believed to be real by millions of otherwise practical-minded Americans.

A career in radio gives opportunities to journalists to write news spots for the medium of sound, to actors to try new approaches to their craft, and to production people and technicians to work in an exciting medium with a future.

The eighties will go down in history as the golden era of sound. Digital recording, the compact disc, and stereo television have been more than technological breakthroughs. They are changing the program preferences of audiences and getting people back into hi-fi listening; they are putting new vigor into an industry that was stagnating.

Music videos, stereo television, and digital recording are opening up new opportunities for audio engineers and entrepreneurs. They account for the recent growth in audio careers. Developments in audio technology and recording techniques have taken the audio profession outside the narrow marketplace of radio stations and expanded the field to such places as soundstage studios and postproduction facilities for video and film.

Many novices to the radio and professional audio field concentrate on mastering the technology. While it is necessary to be good at the craft, it is more important to understand the process of producing sound. You must know the scope and limitations of radio as a medium of mass communication before you produce and transmit programs. You should also understand the principles, aesthetics, techniques, and technology of producing sound before setting forth on a career in professional audio. In the words of Julian Jaynes, "Sound is a very special modality. We cannot handle it. We cannot push it away. We cannot turn our backs to it. We can close our eyes, hold our noses, withdraw from touch, refuse to taste. We cannot close our ears though we can partly muffle them. Sound is the least controllable of all sense modalities."*

## WHERE THE JOBS ARE

Radio stations provide a great variety of jobs for creative and competitive communicators. These jobs are in the areas of announcing, programming, sales, engineering, and management. Radio broadcasters may qualify for several jobs at television stations. Jobs for audio professionals such as *music directors, recording artists, sound mixers,* and *engineers* are available at recording studios and postproduction facilities. In addition, there are an increasing number of jobs for audio professionals at production companies and corporate media departments that produce audio for video and other media. Manufacturers and dealers of high-fidelity sound equipment also provide jobs for those trained in audio.

The Audio Engineering Society (AES) has a membership of more than 10,000 audio engineers, technicians, professors, and students. AES members represent radio and television stations, audio recording studios, video and film production and postproduction companies, manufacturers of sound equipment and dealer shops, and colleges and universities.

---

*Julian Jaynes, *The Origin of Consciousness in the Breakdown of the Bicameral Mind* (Boston: Houghton Mifflin, 1976), pp. 96–97.

**Radio stations**     Radio has long been the most effective medium of mass communications used to disseminate information with immediacy. It is constantly utilized to communicate with people over long as well as short distances. Radio relays news faster and to a greater number of people than any other medium. There are almost 500 million radio sets in the United States. People listen to the radio for news and entertainment in their homes, offices, and cars. The integration of AM channel reception into personal stereo units has made for greater distribution of radio programs.

There are over 10,000 radio stations on the air in the United States. Radio stations offer specialized programming such as classical music, all news, talk shows, and religious broadcasts. The vast majority of stations devote most of their airtime to playing some particular type of music. Specialized programming formats give each radio station a distinctive personality.

National Public Radio (NPR) is a major supplier of programming for educational radio stations. If you are interested in working in educational radio, contact NPR at 2025 M St., NW, Washington, DC 20036.

Working at a radio station can be both exciting and challenging. Your best source for identifying radio stations with specialized programming formats in a particular geographic region is *Broadcasting Yearbook*.

**TV stations**     Job opportunities for broadcasters and audio professionals are available at TV stations. Many television stations hire people with radio experience into positions as newscasters and audio engineers. You can find a listing of television stations in *Broadcasting Yearbook*. For more information on jobs in broadcasting, contact the National Association of Broadcasters (NAB), 1771 North St., NW, Washington, DC 20036.

**Production studios**     Recording studios and production companies that record, sweeten, master, and duplicate audiotape for the recording, broadcast, film, and video industries have job openings for audio pros. The Society of Professional Audio Recording Studios (SPARS) estimates that there are nearly 3,000 production studios in the country. The major recording centers in the United States are in New York; California; Nashville, Tennessee; and Chicago. You can identify facilities in the geographic region of your interest by using *International Recording Equipment and Studio Directory* (New York: Billboard Publications, Inc.), available in the reference section of most local public libraries. Several production companies are contracted by advertising agencies to produce jingles.

**Corporations**     Media departments within corporations utilize audio for video and other media, such as audiovisual presentations. The number of jobs for audio-only specialists in this market segment is limited; however, corporations with large media departments do hire audio engineers and technicians. Universities and colleges with broadcast facilities offer jobs to both programming and technically-trained audio specialists. Some speech and foreign language training organizations, such as the Alliance Francaise, use the services of audio people to produce foreign language learning tapes.

## THE JOBS

The responsibilities and job functions of radio and audio professionals vary considerably, depending on the nature of programming at the radio station or production studio.

**Radio stations**

Job titles in the area of programming include *program manager, music director, music librarian, announcer/DJ* (disc jockey), *production manager, public service director, news writer/editor,* and *scriptwriter.*

Programming tasks at an all-music radio station can be quite simple. Typically, it consists of hour after hour of prerecorded music, interspersed with newscasts and public service announcements (PSAs). At an all-news station, programming can be quite challenging. These stations require the program staff to constantly screen news sources such as United Press International (UPI) audio and edit items of interest for its primary audience group. These jobs call for speed, spontaneity, and flexibility. Several FM radio stations have contract affiliations with a national radio network to air certain programs. Network affiliation is advantageous to radio stations with limited staff, as they receive hourly newscasts and on-the-spot coverage of major events.

**Program director.**   The head of the programming team is the *program director,* who is responsible for a staff of writers, producers, and on-air personalities. Program directors schedule broadcasts on a day-to-day basis and handle staff, schedules, budgets, and license renewal applications.

**Music director.**   The *music director* is responsible for selecting and arranging prerecorded music to fit the station's programming format. An effective music director must appreciate music, share the listening preferences of the station's audience and spend many hours auditioning new records. The music director often doubles as an announcer and must also be able to interview recording stars.

**Music librarian.**   There are a limited number of jobs for music librarians. Typically, this job calls for cataloging and indexing skills.

**Announcers.**   One of the more visible positions at a radio station is that of an *announcer* (or *DJ*). Most radio listeners identify programs by referring to the announcer. Good announcers build a rapport with their audiences and thereby get to be well-known personalities. The job calls for reading commercial copy, interviewing guests, and introducing new recordings.

**Production manager.**   In larger stations, a production manager will have a distinct function of ensuring that programs are aired on schedule. In smaller stations, the functions of program manager and production manager are often combined.

**Public service director.**   The public service director is responsible for ensuring that the station airs PSAs to meet FCC requirements. The public service director must determine community needs and decide which needs call for broadcast exposure. Not all stations hire a separate person for the function of public service or community affairs. Public service responsibilities are frequently assigned to programmer-news directors.

**News department.**   The news department of a radio station is an exciting place to work. The jobs of *news director, writer–editor,* and *reporter* call for keeping on top of major news-breaking events such as political meetings, disasters, and social issues. This department of radio journalists also covers weather and traffic-related news.

You can learn more about radio journalism through the Radio and Television News Directors Association, 1735 DeSalles Street, NW, Washington, DC 20036.

**Scriptwriter.**   Although there are few jobs for a radio scriptwriter per se, a number of stations that air radio dramas and talk shows utilize the talents of good scriptwriters. Scriptwriters who are hired on-staff at radio stations are responsible for preparing continuity copy between programs as well as commercial announcements and PSAs.

**Radio sales.**   Radio stations hire sales staff in the positions of *general sales manager, national* and *local sales managers,* and *radio sales reps.* The responsibility of this department is primarily that of generating revenue for the radio station. It does so by selling advertising time. In any of these positions, you will be required to represent the station and present demographics on its audience to potential advertisers.

**Radio traffic.**   The traffic department is responsible for the preparation of minute-by-minute schedules. Daily schedules contain specific information on what program has to be aired and the precise time of broadcast. A *radio traffic supervisor's* job calls for handling schedule changes and maintaining a close check on all departments to ensure that schedules are met. Larger stations may employ *traffic assistants* to handle such tasks as traffic flow and record keeping. An increasing number of radio stations are automating traffic functions.

**Radio engineering.**   All radio stations employ broadcast engineers and technicians. Radio stations are required to meet government regulations; the engineering department is responsible for this function. The *chief engineer* is responsible for heading the technical operations team. These people install, repair, and maintain studio and transmitter equipment.

**Radio management and administration.**   A *station manager* is responsible for formulating policy and for the overall supervision of the radio station. Within the administration department of a larger station, several jobs are available, such as *personnel director, purchasing manager,* and *security officer.*

**Production studios**

Jobs in this segment of the industry call for a good understanding of sound production and facility in using audio equipment. Audio professionals, who can record, rerecord, do special effects (SFX) mixing, and handle multitrack recording and signal routing can apply for jobs at the numerous production studios in the country.

Some of the job titles in the creative area include the following: *supervisor, rerecording mixers, SFX rerecording mixer, music rerecording mixer, supervisor sound mixers,* and *production sound mixer.*

The listed recording job titles are typically those of audio teams who work on sound tracks for the recording and motion picture industries. These jobs involve the selection and mixing of music and special effects as specified by the producer. They entail "cleaning up" audio tracks of any noise or other disturbing elements. On-location recording jobs call for the appropriate selection of microphones and the effective use of noise-reduction equipment.

Postproduction recording facilities require audio pros to be adept at the audio-sweetening process which involves enhancing the quality of the soundtrack with music, sound effects, and background presence. Technically speaking, an audiotrack is enhanced or sweetened by eliminating noise and disturbance. Sweetening the audiotrack allows the producer to perfect all the audio that was neglected at various stages of the production process. Hollywood-scale productions and many large-budget radio jingles not only mix various sound sources, but often get involved in rebuilding and replacing every audio element in a production.

Audio-for-video calls for mixing and synchronizing the audio elements for the video image. Talented recording artists who work on the creative aspects of audio can aspire for such recognition as the LYRA awards given to Academy Award nominees in the various sound categories each year on the Saturday before the Oscar awards.

Production studios also employ *audio engineers* and *technicians,* whose primary responsibility is maintaining studio and on-location equipment to its optimum specification standards.

Audio engineers are also responsible for the selection of state-of-the-art equipment and are often called upon to be responsible for the design and construction of sound-rooms or "suites," in expanding facilities.

**Corporations**

The only positions in corporate media departments dedicated solely to audio are those of *audio engineers* and *technicians*. The responsibilities that go with these titles in a corporation are similar to those in a production studio. If you are interested in the creative aspects of audio in a corporate media department, you must also acquire visual production skills.

### EDUCATION AND EXPERIENCE

Every year, nearly 20,000 students graduate from radio, television, and communications schools. Most of them seek jobs at radio and TV stations. The broadcast industry, however, can absorb only a limited number of these graduates, thus making entry into the profession competitive and tough.

In the long run, it pays to develop more than one skill that a radio station can utilize. Of the hundreds of schools in the country, more than 350 have departments of telecommunications that offer courses in broadcasting. Several of these departments offer a series of courses in theory and skills development, toward what is frequently referred to as a "broadcast track."

Many colleges operate their own radio stations, thus providing students with the opportunity to gain practical experience. Some junior colleges and community colleges also offer broadcasting courses.

Check the *College Yearbook* for more information on universities and colleges offering broadcast courses. The Association of Education in Journalism and Mass Communications (AEJMC) Catalog will list the sequences that are accredited by AEJMC. You can write to the Broadcast Education Association for a listing of two-year institutions offering broadcast courses.

**Skills for programming**

Radio programming departments require you to have good writing and oral communication skills. You must be able to write effectively for the sound medium. Radio journalists must be adept at gathering news and also have good interviewing skills. As part of the programming team, you will need to develop some technical proficiencies, such as the handling of microphones, turntables, and tape recorders.

As a radio announcer, you will be required to have excellent audio presentation skills. You might want to join a debating society or drama group to train in voice projection and control. It is also necessary to develop the ability to speak *extemporae* and to ad lib. DJs and talk-show announcers are top-notch speakers who have the ability to hold an audience in rapture with their words and voices.

If you are interested in a radio programming career, you should develop strong research skills and also have a broad knowledge of community, national, and international affairs. Your college training should be a good balance between the liberal arts and specific radio-related skills.

Managerial jobs in a radio programming department call for hiring and training newscasters and announcers, scheduling studio and staff, and controlling the budget. Those who aspire to the position of program director would do well to get a master's degree in communications or business and broad experience in broadcasting.

**Skills for radio sales**

A job in the radio sales area of broadcast requires at least a high school diploma, a pleasant personality, and selling abilities. You will need to call on advertisers and advertising agencies to sell "spots." You must be able to do research on audiences and understand ratings, so as to present demographics of audiences to the potential advertisers.

**Skills for radio traffic**

Since various traffic functions are now being automated, it is necessary for traffic supervisors and assistants to have computer skills. A high school education, at least, is necessary for these jobs. Business school training will undoubtedly increase and enhance your job opportunities.

**Skills for radio engineering**

You must have a keen interest in electronics and gadgetry to start a career as a radio engineer or technician. A high school diploma plus technical or trade school courses is necessary for an entry-level job as a radio technician. You must be able to perform a full range of maintenance and repair services.

Many stations prefer to hire technicians with first-class FCC operator's licenses. A chief engineer should have a first-class operator's license and be completely familiar with FCC rules and procedures. To be successful as a radio engineer, you should get a college degree in engineering or two years of technical school training together with extensive experience (at least five years) as a broadcast technician.

**Skills for studio work**

Audio professionals should have a good knowledge of production, postproduction editing, recording, rerecording, and mixing techniques. While recording in a studio, you must have the ability to recognize the limitations of the room design and utilize appropriate techniques to get the best possible recording. You must have the ability to utilize a mixing console or board as well as multichannel consoles. In a nutshell, you must know how to use audio equipment. A number of trade schools offer courses in audio recording, mixing, and signal routing.

**SOURCES OF INFORMATION**

**Associations and Societies**

These organizations have information on careers in radio broadcasting and professional audio. Addresses appear in Appendix A.

Acoustical Society of America (ASA)
American Women in Radio and Television
Audio Engineering Society (AES)
Broadcast Education Association
Institute of Electrical and Electronics Engineers (IEEE)
International Radio and Television Society
National Academy of Recording Arts and Sciences (NARAS)
National Association of Black-Owned Broadcasters
National Association of Broadcasters (NAB)
Radio-Television News Directors Association
Recording Industry Association of America, Inc. (RIAA)
Society of Motion Picture and Television Engineers (SMPTE)
Society of Professional Audio Recording Studios (SPARS)

**Periodicals**

Addresses appear in Appendix B.

*Audio Engineering Society Journal*
*Broadcast Engineering*
*dB, The Sound Engineering Magazine*
*Inside Radio*
*International Musician and Recording World*
*Mix*
*Modern Recording and Music*
*Pro Sound News*
*Radio & Records*
*Radio World*
*Radio Active*
*Recording engineer/producer*
*Religious Broadcasting*
*S & VC (Sound & Video Contractor)*
*Sight and Sound*
*SMPTE Journal*
*Sound Engineer*

*Studio Sound*
*Television/Broadcast Communications*

**Directories**

*Broadcasting Yearbook.* Washington, DC: Broadcasting Publications. Annual.

*The Directory of Religious Broadcasting.* Morristown, NY: National Religious Broadcaster. Annual.

*The Illustrated Audio Equipment Reference Catalog.* Shawnee Mission, KS: Bill Daniels Co. Annual.

*International Recording Equipment and Studio Directory.* New York: Billboard Publications, Inc. Annual.

*Radio Contacts.* New York: Larimi Communications Associates. Annual.

*Television Cable Factbook: The Authoritative Reference for Television, Cable Electronics Industries.* 2 vols. Washington, DC: Television Digest. Annual.

**Recommended Reading**

Baskerville, David. *Music Business Handbook & Career Guide.* 5th ed. Denver: Sherwood, 1990.

Clifford, Martin. *Microphones.* 3rd ed. Blue Ridge Summit, PA: Tab Books, 1986.

Dudek, Lee J. *Professional Broadcast Announcing.* Boston: Allyn and Bacon, 1982.

Eargle, John. *The Microphone Handbook.* Plainview, NY: ELAR, 1981.

Edmonds, Robert. *The Sights and Sounds of Cinema and Television.* New York: Teachers College Press, 1982.

Everest, F. Alton. *Critical Listening: An Audio Training Course* (Manual and Tapes). Thousand Oaks, CA: SIE Publishing, 1982.

_____ . *The Master Handbook of Acoustics.* Blue Ridge Summit, PA: Tab Books, 1981.

McLeish, Robert. *The Technique of Radio Production.* 2nd ed. Boston: Focal Press, 1988.

Martin, George. *All You Need Is Ears.* New York: St. Martin's Press, 1982.

O'Donnell, Lewis B., Philip Benoit, and Carl Hausman. *Modern Radio Production.* 2nd ed. Belmont, CA: Wadsworth, 1990.

Oringel, Robert. *Audio Control Handbook.* 5th ed. New York: Hastings House, 1983.

Rapaport, Diane Sward. *How to Make and Sell Your Own Record.* 3rd ed. San Francisco: Headlands Press, 1988.

Runstein, Robert. *Modern Recording Techniques.* 3rd ed. Indianapolis: H. W. Sams, 1989.

Stephens, Mitchell. Broadcast News: *Radio Journalism and an Introduction to Television*. 2nd ed. New York: Holt, Rinehart and Winston, 1986.

Truax, Barry. *Acoustic Communication*. Norwood, NJ: Ablex, 1985.

Woodward, Walt. *An Insider's Guide to Advertising Music*. New York: Art Directions Book Co., 1982.

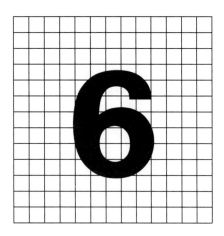

# MULTIMEDIA

The audiovisual communicator is a blend of artisan and technician, with a little magician thrown in.*

---

*Billy Bowles, address at the Audiovisual Congress, Photokina, Cologne, Germany, 1986.

Multimedia and audiovisual communications career opportunities are growing in business, medicine, government, education, religion, and advertising/public relations agencies, as well as independent media production companies. The audiovisual practitioner, once thought of as a technician, is gaining status in these organizations as an audiovisual communicator. With this status has come greater recognition and higher salaries.

The end of the industrial age signaled the beginning of the information age. In this age of information, audiovisual communication has experienced tremendous growth. All publics today are demanding more information: employees, customers, and stockholders, to name a few.

Stockholders meetings which used to be dull, annual, required formalities are now more often than not media extravaganzas. They are choreographed by audiovisual professionals. Multi-image shows dramatize the company's achievements. The photography is impressive, the narrator believable, the music and sound effects supportive, and most important, the message is clear. The CEO (chief executive officer) is lighted in a manner that accentuates her or his importance and best personal features. The latest in computerized audiovisual equipment is used to present the program. It takes a team of audiovisual professionals to produce such an event. In the 1970s, at the same meeting, an overhead projector may have been the only display device present.

The audiovisual and multimedia professionals who create these events have a host of media to choose from with which to communicate. They skillfully use charts and graphs in their presentations, incorporate still photography and film, supplement with computer graphics and video, and enhance with a variety of music and other audio components.

While stockholder meetings and product introductions may be the most extravagant use of multimedia, audiovisuals are routinely used for all the classic communications purposes.

Videotape has become a significant force and its use in industry is still growing. Especially with computer-generated or computer-controlled images, the use of video is now widespread. However, the 35mm slide is by far the most used medium for communications in industry today. The use of computer graphics and the creative display and manipulation of the 35mm slides with computer-controlled multiple projectors have enhanced its effectiveness and helped prolong its dominance.

## WHERE THE JOBS ARE

**Business and Industry**

There are more audiovisual career opportunities in business and industry than in any other field. Within these businesses, the majority of jobs are located in the corporate communications or public relations departments. The jobs function well here since these departments traditionally work vertically and horizontally throughout the organization. Internal and external communications is their charter.

Internally, business graphics displayed on 35mm color slides and overhead transparencies are by far the most used media. These slides and transparencies are mainly produced for speaker support. In the past, these graphics were prepared as flat art and then photographed. Today, however, computer-generated graphics are becoming commonplace, the preferred kind of business graphics.

The Gartner Group states that the average manager spends 59 percent of her or his time in meetings. A Wharton Study reported that use of visuals effectively reduces the duration of meetings by an average of 28 percent. Additional research shows that 85 percent of the people who both see and hear something remember it three hours later, and 65 percent remember it three days later. With the increase in productivity and retention brought on by the use of well-prepared graphics, business executives now have bottom-line reasons for hiring and expanding their audiovisual facilities.

Some businesses have created special environments within which to display or showcase their presentations. It is not uncommon to find boardrooms and company theaters equipped with rear-screened projection, multi-image capability. Very sophisticated, twelve- to fifteen-projector stereo programs can be easily shown. This controlled environment is ideal for making sales presentations to clients or telling your story to a client or public whom you wish to persuade. Having a sophisticated facility to work in and produce programs for is a rewarding experience for the audiovisual professional.

Most large companies have one or more training departments that require audiovisual materials. Major training areas include management development, sales support, and technical training. Certain industries also maintain large customer training activities. Often, each training area may have its own audiovisual crew, although typically, film and video production, if not purchased from vendors, will be centralized. Slides and overheads are a big requirement for training. Poster-size photographs may frequently be requested. Micro- and macrophotography are also often required to show students objects that cannot be seen easily in the classroom.

Marketing departments are big users of audiovisual materials. Some companies participate in numerous trade shows. Here the AV person may be not only required to produce the AV program and photographs that support it but also to accompany the show, set it up, and run it. This may be no easy task, since it can be difficult to control your environment at a trade show. It requires special skills. It might also require a lot of travel and time away from home. This appeals to some but is a burden to others.

The motivational sales meeting is an important audiovisual task in some companies. Amway Corporation, for example, annually produces four such major programs. For this kind of program, the AV professional has a chance to use virtually every audiovisual production skill available and still get assistance from outside vendors who specialize in this type of event. Lasers, dancers, musicians, and singers may be staged with multi-image and video. The entire event may be transmitted via satellite to multiple locations across the country or the world. Working on a project of this magnitude can be a truly rewarding experience. Coordination and good planning skills are the keys to success.

Whether you are working in a small company or a large one will usually determine if you will have the opportunity to specialize or be expected to be an AV generalist; you are likely to be expected to have a wide variety of AV skills. A balance of photography, audio, programming, graphics, and writing talents is needed, so you can handle most tasks as they arise.

**Employment atmosphere.**    Some people are not cut out to work in the corporate world or industry. They may be turned off by the bureaucracy and process-oriented atmosphere prevalent in many companies. A simple requirement like wearing a coat and tie or a tailored dress may not suit your lifestyle. The routine of working nine to five and arriving on time every morning is not everyone's cup of tea. If any of this concerns you, maybe you should consider finding a position in an area that more closely meets your needs sociologically and psychologically.

Working in audiovisuals in business may be a dead end for you if you are career-oriented. Certainly, if you desire to be a vice president or officer in a company, AV is not the path to take; in that case, you need to pursue a management track, and audiovisuals is not a part of it. Within the audiovisual department, advancement may be limited because of the relatively small size of the group; to get ahead someone must move or the department expand. Turnover or attrition may be your most likely possibility for advancement; however, turnover is not uncommon in this discipline.

**Health Science**

You have only to look around in your own city and see the number of hospitals and other medical facilities located there to realize that you may not have to travel far to practice your audiovisual skills. If you also have an aptitude or interest in the medical field, a job in this area could be satisfying to you. In addition to hospitals, AV job opportunities are available at medical, dental, nursing, and veterinary schools and universities. Pharmaceutical companies should also not be overlooked.

Teaching hospitals are the most likely to have entry-level AV jobs. They are generally good places to start your career, as the AV department staff size is usually small and requires each member to get involved in all aspects of audiovisuals. The job includes shooting thousands of slides from operations to copywork for use in doctors' lectures and documentation. Because of confidentiality and the need for quick turnaround, many hospitals process their own film, making them good places to learn another procedure.

Productions using slides and slide photography are the largest medium in health science audiovisuals. To work in this field, you should be motivated by the challenge of documenting events and objects in a scientific manner and not necessarily in a creative manner. Procedures are established for every function, and you must follow these procedures. Special training in colorimetry is helpful, since color is so important in diagnostics for the physician. The hours are long, you will always be busy, and the pay is usually low; but it can be an excellent learning environment. There should be great satisfaction in knowing that you serve as an integral part of a health care team.

**Government**

Do not overlook federal, state, and local government departments when searching for AV jobs. The state and local government agencies most likely to use AV are agriculture, tourism, police/fire (emergency services), environmental/conservation, game and fish, health/education/welfare, and highway and safety. AV media are used for promotion, information dissemination, and training.

The federal government, according to the Hope Report, has 462 production operations within the defense agencies. Defense is the largest user; the Air Force, Army, Navy, and Marine Corps are each individually larger users of AV than any of the civilian agencies, which number 35. Government use of media is mainly for training, but there is a growing use of slides and overheads for speaker support.

**Religious organizations**

Churches that telecast their worship services have communication specialists on staff who organize and produce the telecasts. Much of the production crew is usually volunteer help. The specialist is often responsible for audiovisual production as well, but the emphasis in churches is on video.

Christian publishing companies sometimes have AV producers on staff that work with independent AV facilities to produce slide/tape programs that visualize the music they publish. This may include text of music superimposed over appropriate slides. These programs are sold to churches to use in their liturgy. Religious education programs are also produced to inform congregations about mission work and other related subjects. Religious organizations do not offer a bevy of full-time jobs but do look for volunteers.

**Independent Media Production Companies**

If you believe variety is the spice of life, then you should seek out an independent media production company to work for. Since their client base is universal, you certainly will most always have something new and different to work on. This can be very challenging, with each project bringing new opportunities and new problems to solve.

It is difficult to gain a position as an AV producer at an independent production company. A *producer* would be expected to have several years of experience and a list of awards to prove talent. Jobs tend to be more specialized in these facilities. They have *audio engineers, photographers,* and *graphics persons* who exercise only specific skills. This is especially true in large companies. It is possible to find assistant-level jobs in these facilities, but those too are highly competitive.

Production facilities stress creativity. They usually have larger production budgets than in-house AV facilities. Job security in independent facilities is not as good as an in-house corporate facility. Independent production companies depend solely on AV production income, while corporations have a broader base of revenues.

**Advertising and Public Relations Agencies**

The jobs at advertising and public relations agencies are limited, since most agencies rely on independent production facilities for their audiovisual production needs. They may have a producer on staff who works with outside production facilities to meet AV and video production needs.

Ad and PR agencies need top quality work, due to the nature of their business. When an agency is pitching a new client, it wants to be perceived as the best competitor. It wants to take advantage of the latest in technological hardware, design, and software in order to impress the client. The agency is selling its expertise and must be presented in the most effective manner available.

## THE JOBS

It is important to realize that teamwork is critical to the success of an audiovisual facility. Jobs and responsibilities overlap and complement each other.

Julie Thomas–Haskell, AV professional at St. Vincent Hospital and Medical Center in Portland, Oregon, describes her facility, "We don't work alone. Medigraphics [the name of her department] is more than a roster of talented individuals, more than a list of skills and equipment." The team includes Ms. Thomas–Haskell, a video specialist, a graphics coordinator, a graphics artist, a typesetter, a medical photographer, a photojournalist, a darkroom assistant, a surgical videographer, and a media clerk who join forces and form a team from start to finish of a project.

**AV Producer**

The *AV producer* is responsible for the design, production, and evaluation of multimedia information and training programs for various audiences. Style, originality, and creativity are extremely important characteristics for a producer. The AV producer acts as resource person for people in the organization with communication needs. Producers assist in achieving clients' objectives within established budgets, in a timely manner, using the appropriate audiovisual hardware to best deliver the presentation.

In the process of preparing single audiovisual presentations, producers use managerial skills—planning, budgeting, leading others, and directing—as well as a wide variety of technical audiovisual skills—doing research, scriptwriting and editing, storyboarding, arranging and doing photography, film processing, lighting, selecting music, recording and mixing audio tracks, designing graphics, programming slides, and operating all kinds of AV equipment.

Leadership and innovativeness are key to a producer's success, and interpersonal skills are important. Producers must be able to guide and bring excitement to the production team, keep emotions and budgets under control in short-deadline situations, and meet each client's objectives.

Producers must understand the capabilities of each of the different kinds of AV equipment—slide projectors, film projectors, overhead projectors, dissolvers, audio tape players, and videocassette recorders—and be able to choose the best format for the assignment at hand. In addition to media production skills, computer literacy is a must. The ultimate job of the producer is to edit large amounts of information and visuals into a comprehensive and succinct program.

**AV Writer**

The work of an *AV writer* involves consultations with the producer and the client from program concept to completion. AV writers must be able to develop innovative scripts through research and consultation, to assure quality programs that meet stated objectives.

The AV writer must be able to perform the same tasks as any other writer: research (using both libraries and computer databases), in-person and telephone interviews, typing or word processing, and correct use of the language (including grammar, spelling, punctuation, syntax, and sentence structure). Additionally, working in the AV medium requires familiarity with a variety of slide, videotape, multi-image, and audio formats and capabilities, plus the ability to write narratives and dialogue in a lively and interesting way.

Writers are the unsung heroes of AV production teams. While they are not as visible as most other members of the production team, their scripts are the foundation of any program. The script is the catalyst for all the visual and aural elements of the program.

## Production Assistant

*Production assistants* get involved in every area of production, including photography, lighting, audio, programming and presentation, and display of the program. Production assistants must have many of the skills required of producers, especially the mechanical ability to work all of the various kinds of AV equipment available.

A production assistant must have a "team attitude," good interpersonal skills, and the flexibility and resourcefulness to deal with changing priorities during the course of a project. He or she must be willing to take direction from the producer and still have the self-confidence to offer creative suggestions and work independently to get things done. This position is a steppingstone on the way to becoming a producer.

## AV Technician

An *AV technician* operates and maintains photographic, audio, lighting, programming, and projection equipment. Maintenance of high technical standards calls for the development of routine equipment maintenance procedures that assure optimum performance levels of all AV equipment in the department or company. As audiovisual hardware becomes increasingly complex, technicians have to be training continually. Technicians may be called on to assist in any phase of production or postproduction.

Basic knowledge of electronics and strong mechanical ability are essential to AV technicians. Experience operating all kinds of AV equipment, computers, and maintenance tools is the basis of the job. Also important is the ability to organize a work schedule and make priorities carefully, as well as to develop and maintain a record of work done on each piece of equipment.

The job of an AV technician is technical in nature and is critical to the operation of the AV department or company. Production schedules have to be delayed or cancelled if equipment is not working properly, because the quality of images produced (if any can be produced) are substandard. When the AV technician is doing the job properly, the production people can concern themselves with the creative use of the equipment and not the ability of the equipment itself to function.

**AV Manager/Director**

The *AV manager* or *director* is responsible for establishing, budgeting, promoting, planning, scheduling, producing, and distributing audiovisual programs so that they meet stated objectives and overcome the obstacles of time, distance, space, and repetition. The qualities most important in an AV manager are strong managerial skills: leadership, organization, control and follow-up, budgeting, research and evaluation, communication, decisiveness, flexibility, and creativity. The manager must use all of these skills to assume a leadership role by promoting the benefits of proper media usage.

The manager of an AV department or company develops professional staff and procures the equipment needed to produce quality programs. He or she exercises final authority on all programs produced and the equipment purchased for use in their production. The manager maintains a production schedule that effectively utilizes human and mechanical resources, and a systematic program evaluation plan to measure program effectiveness.

### EDUCATION AND EXPERIENCE

Education requirements for AV producers, production assistants, and writers are very similar. All require a bachelor's degree, preferably in mass communications (although a journalism, English, or other liberal arts degree might also be adequate), and the basic liberal arts education that goes with such a degree. Having a broad knowledge of the world, its technologies and its cultures, gives business communicators in any field a strong foundation for their work. Certain businesses and industries also look for a strong technical background in their own field. Writing is a particularly important skill to develop, not only for prospective AV writers but also for producers and others who work with the writers.

Internships can give you some practical work experience while you are still in college; the ability to say that you have hands-on experience with the widest possible variety of equipment will serve you well when you are job-hunting. Audiovisual conferences and seminars can also be helpful, giving you a feel for the industry as a whole and keeping you abreast of the latest technologies and trends—not to mention giving you the opportunity to meet people who might eventually hire you.

An AV manager or director needs the same basic skills and education that any AV producer or writer needs, plus fairly extensive experience and a business-oriented approach to the work. Management skills are the key here, whether acquired through college coursework or tough, on-the-job experience. A master's degree in business may be important for advancement in some corporate environments.

Training for AV technicians is a little different than that required for the other jobs discussed here. The technician can get most of the required training for equipment maintenance by attending a vocational school that specializes in electronics. A good background in the theory of electronics and the mechanical ability and knowledge of troubleshooting techniques are essential. Technicians need to continue their education while on the job, attending seminars and training sessions sponsored by equipment manufacturers.

## SOURCES OF INFORMATION

Multi-media/audiovisual communication is a challenging and exciting field for resourceful people who work well under pressure and short deadlines and who are comfortable balancing many tasks at once. There is great reward in having successfully visualized a very complex, dry, and normally dull subject or procedure in a comprehensive manner.

If you are a conceptualizer, a visual thinker and want to work hard to learn the tricks of the trade, a career in multi-media/audiovisual communications may be for you.

**Associations**

Addresses are included in Appendix A.

Association for Educational Communications and Tech (AECT)
Association of Audio-Visual Technicians (AAVT)
Association for Multi-Image International, Inc.
Association of Visual Communicators
Audio Visual Management Association (AVMA)
Catholic A-V Educators Association (CAVE)
Health Education Media Association (HEMA)
Health Sciences Communications Association (HeSCA)
Independent Media Producers Association, Inc. (IMPA)
International Association of Business Communicators (IABC)
International Communications Industries Association (ICIA)
National Computer Graphics Association (NCGA)

## PERIODICALS

You will find addresses for the following periodicals of interest in Appendix B.

*AV Video*
*Communications Concepts*

*Fast Forward*
*Hope Reports*
*Mac User*
*Mac World*
*Media Methods*
*Multi-Images Journal*
*CD-ROM Professional*
*CD-ROM World*
*Computer Pictures*
*Imaging Magazine*
*New Media*
*T.H.E Journal*

## RECOMMENDED READING

Brown, J.W., R.B. Lewis, and F.F. Harcleroad. *AV Instruction: Technology, Media and Methods.* 6th ed. New York: McGraw-Hill Book Company, 1982.

Markle, Susan M. *Good Frames and Bad: A Grammar of Frame Writing.* 2nd ed. New York: John Wiley & Sons, 1969.

National Audio Visual Association. *Audio Visual Equipment Directory.* Fairfax, VA: NAVA.

Schmid, William T. *Media Center Management: A Practical Guide.* New York: Hastings House Publishers, 1980.

Eastman Kodak publishes a series of pamphlets on the planning and preparation of audiovisual and multi-image productions:

Kenny, Michael F. and Schmitt, Raymond F., *Images, Images: The Book of Programmed Multi-Image Production.*
*Effective Visual Presentations.*
*Materials for Visual Presentations: Planning and Preparation.*
*Planning and Producing Slide Programs.*
*Printing Color Slides and Larger Transparencies.*
*Slides with a Purpose.*
*Synchronizing a Slide/Tape Program.*
*Wide-Screen and Multiple-Screen Presentations.*

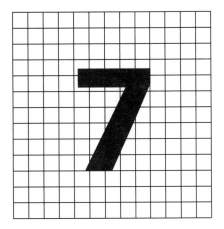

# TELEVISION AND VIDEO

With much of television's potential still to be realized, there is little danger of stagnation for those who make it their life's work.*

---

*"Your Career in Television," Television Information Office, 1985.

Television is the youngest, yet most powerful, medium of communication we have today. Its ability to grab the viewer, both emotionally and intellectually, has made it emerge as the dominant mass media communications channel of our time. It is, in fact, the all-pervasive medium—the instant informer, effective teacher, primary persuader, and great entertainer.

Television has dramatically changed the nature of news. It has given us the ability to deliver news as it happens—instantly, accurately, and vividly. Television as a teacher has revolutionized our traditional concept of education. It allows us the opportunity to make learning interactive and interesting. The persuasive power of television messages commands billions of advertising dollars annually. Television motivates consumers to buy, politicians to mold public opinion, and preachers to spread "the Word." And indeed, television seems to have tremendous influence upon our society in an infinite variety of ways.

Rapid technological advances in the television industry have widened the scope of its application to all sectors of society. Breakthroughs in satellite and transmission systems have given broadcasters the ability to conduct international teleconferences. The proliferation of new cable channels has led to a cable penetration of more than a third of the nearly 85 million TV households in the United States. Advances in production distribution equipment, e.g., Electronic News Gathering (ENG) systems and the laser devices, such as the videodisc player have led to greater use of television by organizations. Innovations in product design have made cameras and videocassette recorders (VCRs) smaller and more affordable for home use. This widespread use of television has led to a multi-billion dollar industry, generating employment opportunities in the performing, production, administrative, marketing, and technical areas.

## WHERE THE JOBS ARE

**Broadcast Television**

The Federal Communications Commission (FCC) makes channel assignments. Some 2,000 channels are in operation in 1,300 communities. Nearly two thirds of the channel allocations are to commercial stations. Hence, the majority of television jobs in the broadcast industry are available at commercial stations. The largest commercial TV networks are *Columbia Broadcasting Services* (CBS) Corporation, *National Broadcasting Corporation* (NBC), and *American Broadcasting Corporation* (ABC). These three networks have corporate headquarters in New York and studio facilities in Manhattan, Los Angeles, and other major cities worldwide. They have news operations in several cities nationwide. Networks generate original programming and therefore provide tremendous job opportunities for creative, administrative, and technical personnel.

Many commercial television stations are affiliated with networks and receive their programs via microwave or satellite transmissions; such stations are known as *network affiliates*. Some commercial television stations are not affiliated with a network; such a station is commonly referred to as an *independent TV station*. Independents use a variety of sources for programming. While it is not uncommon for an independent station to rely heavily on the use of motion pictures and reruns of programs previously shown on the networks, many of them also generate local news and other original programming. Several nationally known broadcasters began their careers at independent stations.

The *Public Broadcasting System* (PBS) is the largest noncommercial network in the United States. It has studio facilities in major cities. It provides national programming and research to PBS-affiliated educational TV stations. Noncommercial educational channel assignments are also made to colleges, universities, and community groups. The FCC makes 242 channel assignments for noncommercial educational use. Some universities and religious institutions that have television channels provide job opportunities for producers and technicians.

A good source for a listing of television networks is the *Broadcasting-Cablecasting Yearbook*. Published annually by Broadcasting Publications, Inc., it is a comprehensive directory of firms that develop and market all types of radio and television news services, video programs, and films.

**Cable Television**

Several communities are outside the broadcast areas of networks, affiliates, and independent TV stations. In an attempt to serve these communities, *cable television* (CATV) stations pick up programs from satellites, or off the air from individual TV stations, by using a powerful central receiving antenna or microwave relay system. The programs are then delivered to the homes of subscribers via coaxial cable.

Cable franchises have currently been issued to nearly 18,500 communities. FCC regulations require CATV stations that serve over 3,500 subscribers to originate a certain amount of programming. Hence, there are some creative programming jobs at the 3,700 stations that produce some programs in their own studios. But, by and large, cable TV systems operate with small staffs. The *National Cable Television Association* reports approximately 40,000 persons employed in the cable industry. Most of the jobs are for cable operators and franchisers and program suppliers. Many opportunities also exist for experienced sales and technically qualified personnel. The few creative opportunities in the cable industry are at the local level—local news, local sports, and programs of interest to the local community.

**Corporate Television**

Corporations as well as nonprofit institutions use television extensively to communicate with and train staff, and to advertise and promote products and services. The majority of corporate and institutional applications of television are not broadcast. Hence, this sector of the industry has been called *industrial television, nonbroadcast television, corporate television*, and *private television* in the past. *Organizational TV* is the new name that is emerging, though not yet widely used. The field of organizational television embraces all businesses—manufacturing, trading and services industries, as well as not-for-profit institutions, such as hospitals, universities, and museums.

Some corporations have small television departments—there are quite a few one-person shops. Many organizational television departments are outgrowths of AV departments. Television in several large companies is a function of the communications or media department. Since television is widely used for training within corporations, it is often part of the human resources department.

Large corporations are using new television technologies (such as teleconferencing and interactive video) to meet some of their complex communication needs. Johnson & Johnson conducted a nationwide press conference via teleconference to announce the reintroduction of Tylenol. Tektronix, Inc. conducted a six-hour technical training through a teleconference; the one-way video, two-way audio session introduced two new Tektronix instruments to its 200 U.S. sales engineers. Hospital Satellite Network produced and transmitted *Who Cares for the Poor,* a 90-minute video conference in which 200 hospitals examined the position of the federal government on this issue.

While the single largest application of videodisc technology has been training, today it is increasingly being used at point-of-sale and for archival purposes. For example, Doyle Dane Bernbach uses videodiscs for storage of commercials. J.P. Stevens & Company designed an online interactive video system for point-of-sale. This electronic system which allows the customer to view Stevens' entire line of bed and bath products was installed in seven of its major department stores in Boston, Washington DC, and Dallas. At the World Exposition '84 in Louisiana, the U.S. pavilion featured an electronic aquarium display in which a videodisc program created interactive "fish tanks."

The development of the half-inch cassette recorder has led to the expansion of corporate TV departments into corporate video networks. Half-inch video as a distribution medium has made it possible for corporations to communicate with their branch offices. At Toyota, for example, five departments make use of the video network for customer relations, service merchandising, sales, parts, and technical training. Schlumberger has an international video network of over 300 units used primarily for technical training.

This phenomenal growth in organizational television is due, in part, to technological developments, to the creative and dynamic production techniques used by private television producers, and to the challenge and spirit of competitiveness generated at professional video competitions.

The foremost industry association in the organizational TV area is the *International Television Association* (ITVA). Its members represent corporations, health, medical, and educational institutions; video production and postproduction companies; and manufacturers, dealers, and distributors of television equipment. Many of these companies have full-fledged video departments staffed by managers, producers, directors, writers, designers, engineers, and technicians. The ITVA membership directory is an excellent source of information on organizations currently using television. The association also offers its members a job information exchange service.

## Government Television

The largest government-operated broadcast enterprise is *Armed Forces Radio and Television Services* (AFRTS). It operates more than 800 radio and television stations in 50 nations worldwide. In some cities, AFRTS operates out of conventional broadcast stations; in others it has closed-circuit television (CCTV) operations. AFRTS employs both military and civilian personnel to operate its television facilities and create programming.

Other government departments also utilize television extensively, though not all of them broadcast programs. Some government departments generate their own programming; others contract independent production companies to develop programs. For example, four major production companies were involved in the production of a multidisciplinary laser videodisc and television project entitled *The World of Work,* commissioned by the Center for Libraries and Education Improvement at the United States Department of Education. The *Directory of U.S. Government Audiovisual Personnel,* published by the National Audiovisual Center in Washington DC, is a good lead to federal agencies with television/video jobs.

**Production Companies**

Many corporate TV departments cannot produce in-house all the video programs needed by the company. They often contract independent producers to script, shoot, and edit programs. Some institutions with limited in-house production equipment use the facilities of production and postproduction companies like Unitel in New York and One Pass Video in Los Angeles. These companies offer state-of-the-art production and postproduction equipment, such as digital video effects (DVE) systems, computer-generated video graphics and paint systems, and services such as film-to-tape transfers, audio sweetening, and videotape duplication. Many television commercials are produced by production companies or independent producers who edit and master the tape at a post facility.

Job opportunities are available at production and postproduction companies. *The Video Register* lists these facilities by state. Each listing includes company name, address, telephone/telex number, and personnel where appropriate. The *Producer's Masterguide,* which lists postproduction facilities, film and video labs, and sound/stage studios, is also a good reference.

## THE JOBS

**Broadcast Television**

In the broadcast industry, job titles and responsibilities are classified into five areas: program-production, news, sales, engineering, and administration. At a small station, one might be called upon to handle a wide variety of assignments. At a large station, job functions are more specialized. A small station environment is the best way to develop versatility. The more jobs you are able to do well, the better and faster your chances of career advancement.

**Program production.**   Some of the job titles at a TV station are *program manager, operations manager, television producer, TV director, TV production assistant, scriptwriter, floor manager, set and props manager, art director, TV tape-film manager, TV staff announcer,* and *research director.* Each of these jobs has discrete functions and responsibilities. For example, a *program manager* needs a thorough knowledge of how the entire station operates. In particular, he or she must have the skills and experience necessary to supervise the production staff, as well as the ability to create, select, and purchase programs. The *operations manager* coordinates and supervises the efforts of both the commercial and noncommercial program departments scheduled for telecast, on a day-to-day basis. A television producer may often double as a TV director; job functions with both titles include planning and directing all the creative aspects of putting together a live or taped production. Responsibilities include overseeing the progress of script, set, props, lighting, sound and budget, and of course you will "call the shots" during production.

**Television news.**   The networks employ broadcast journalists and television production people such as video editors. The emphasis on news at any station can scarcely be overstated. This is due, in large part, to the increase in local television news coverage. With the growth of cable, there is more narrowcasting aimed at audiences with specific or special information needs. While sports, weather forecasts, and traffic reports are regularly covered as specific news items, new special interest topics such as farm reports, consumer economics, health, and science are receiving local news coverage.

While the job opportunities in television news during the past decade grew dramatically, today's automated newsroom is restricting employment growth.

Job titles in television news departments include *TV news director, TV managing editor, TV news producer-director, TV news production assistant, TV news reporter,* and *TV newscaster.* Television news gathering and reporting is both an exciting and demanding job, and you must be a trained broadcast journalist for a job in this sector of the industry.

A TV news director has overall responsibility for a news team of reporters, writers, editors, and newscasters, as well as the studio and mobile unit production crew. The job involves quick decision-making abilities, especially in situations yielding fast-breaking news.

TV news reporting is both glamorous and challenging. For an on-camera news reporter's job, you must have good investigative and presentation skills.

**Television sales.**   Job titles in the sales divisions of television stations include *TV general sales manager, national sales manager, sales service coordinator, TV traffic supervisor,* and *media coordinator.* Jobs in this area deal with the sale of on-air television time. The networks and independent stations derive revenue from the sale of time for announcements (commercials) and program sponsorships.

Sales reps or managers need dynamic selling skills. They must have the ability to use research and audience demographics effectively in a sales presentation to media buyers. As an entry-level job in television, sales does not require more than a high school diploma; many people use it to "get a foot in the door," and then move on to the creative departments of television news and program production.

**Engineering.**   The quality of video and audio signals transmitted by a station depends on its engineering and technical staff. Job titles in this department include *TV chief engineer, assistant chief engineer, TV technical director,* and *audio engineer.* These engineering jobs require that you have technical training and considerable experience. The positions call for regular checks and maintenance of studio cameras, film projectors, video and audio tape recorders, remote relay equipment, mobile units, transmitters, and other television equipment. A job as chief engineer or assistant chief engineer requires a first-class operator's license and several years of experience in television engineering.

If you are electronically inclined and want to start your career as a broadcast technician, you should first get some technical training. You can, however, start your career with minimal technical training and an apprenticeship. The best way to get an entry-level position is to be willing to work as an apprentice technician. It is also an excellent way to learn the job and move ahead with increased ability to take on greater responsibility.

**Administration.**   Job titles in the area of administration include *general manager, TV station manager, TV business manager,* and *manager of office services.* These managerial positions call for establishing policy and setting guidelines for the staff. Managers must have a knowledge of strategic planning and a good business sense. General managers make decisions regarding the purchase of syndicated programs and prepare the station's application for FFC renewal, among other things.

Administrative jobs require a familiarity with broadcast law and experience at negotiating with unions. In addition, you must have excellent leadership qualities and a good public presence. Top-level administrative jobs are acquired through years of experience in various sectors of the television industry by those who demonstrate outstanding managerial qualities.

**Corporate Television**   Job titles, functions, and responsibilities in a corporate media department can be classified into production, management, and technical areas.

**Production.**   All the creative activities of television production fall in this area. Job functions include scriptwriting, lighting, graphics and titles preparation, set design, camera operation, videotape editing, special effects generation, audio sweetening, and the duplication and distribution of videotapes.

In a corporate media department, job titles may overlap several functions. For example, it is unlikely that you would be hired as an on-staff scriptwriter without other responsibilities. If you are a *scriptwriter* with TV production abilities, a company may hire you as a *writer-producer.* Since the majority of corporate TV programs are used for training, writers and producers must be familiar with instructional design procedures. As a scriptwriter, you would be involved in conducting a needs analysis, researching the content, determining the objectives, and selecting the appropriate script format for the proposed program.

A *producer-director* is responsible for the design, production, distribution, and evaluation of the videotaped programs and the few live television programs (such as a teleconference) a corporation conducts. Job functions include controlling and directing talent and crew during video productions. A corporate TV producer must have up-to-date knowledge of production techniques and hands-on experience in the use of state-of-the-art video equipment.

**Management.**  A *media resource director* is responsible for the overall establishment, promotion, planning, production, and distribution of television. This job entails reviewing company reports, policies, and procedures, and recommending the use of television when it can serve as an effective communications tool. This job also includes staffing and budgeting responsibilities.

**Technical.**  The TV engineering and technical staff is responsible for the purchase, maintenance, and replacement of capital equipment. Responsibilities include maintaining the technical standards of color television equipment, doing trouble-shooting and repair on a day-to-day basis.

### EDUCATION AND EXPERIENCE

A high school diploma is a bare minimum qualification for an entry-level job in any sector of the television industry. As this is a highly competitive industry, college education is becoming increasingly important. You will increase your chances of obtaining employment and advancing to a higher position through advanced training.

Traditionally, television courses at undergraduate schools have focused on subjects that give students an understanding of how the broadcast industry operates. In addition to basic television production skills, students are taught to consider ratings, markets, advertising strategies, and broadcast laws and regulations. Over 300 four-year colleges offer broadcast courses.

In recent years, the more forward-thinking educational institutions in the country have incorporated nonbroadcast corporate or organizational television courses into the telecommunications program. Nearly 150 four-year colleges offer courses in nonbroadcast communications. Some junior colleges, like the Borough of Manhattan Community College in New York, have designed comprehensive programs to prepare students for jobs in corporations or in the cable television industry. Nonbroadcast or industrial television courses put an emphasis on planning, scheduling, and budgeting procedures, as well as video production skills. Since a large number of corporate television programs are used for training, these courses also focus on industrial design and program evaluation.

Although most universities have been slow in responding to the need for special training, caused by the rapid growth in the cable industry, some colleges offer one or two cable-related courses. The cable industry needs people who understand franchising and financing. In addition, you must know how cable audiences are targeted and measured, and how programs are rated.

In the television industry at large, there is a real shortage of technical people. With rapid developments in technology, trained and experienced technicians are hard to find. While not all TV engineering or technical maintenance and repair jobs require a formal degree in engineering, most of them call for technical school training and on-the-job experience. Technical training can be acquired at engineering schools, technical colleges, community colleges, manufacturer-sponsored workshops, and through in-service training.

**Broadcast Television**

Since jobs in the broadcast industry can be roughly classified into management/administrative; news/programming; advertising/sales; and technical areas, you should first identify the area in which you would like to build your career.

**Professional Video Programs in Higher Education**

The following list of four year institutions with professional video programs was compiled for the International Television Association by Michael J. Porter, Ph.D. and Barton L. Griffith, Ph.D., Department of Speech and Dramatic Art, University of Missouri-Columbia.

**Four Year Institutions with Professional Video Programs**

| | | | |
|---|---|---|---|
| *Concordia Univ. Loyola | CAN | *Florida State Univ. | FL |
| Arkansas College | AR | West Florida Univ. | FL |
| Arkansas State Univ. | AR | Morehouse College | GA |
| *University of Laverne | CA | Shorter College | GA |
| *San Jose State Univ. | CA | *Northern Iowa Univ. | IA |
| Chapman College | CA | Drake University | IA |
| *Pepperdine Univ. | CA | University of Idaho | ID |
| *CA Institute of Arts | CA | Columbia College | IL |
| California State Univ. | CA | Eastern Illinois Univ. | IL |
| De Anza College | CA | *Governors State Univ. | IL |
| *California State | CA | *Wheaton College | IL |
| *San Francisco State | CA | College of DuPage | IL |
| *Colorado State Univ. | CO | *NE Illinois Univ. | IL |
| University of Colorado, Boulder | CO | Quincy College | IL |
| Metropolitan State Col. | CO | Ball State University | IN |
| *University of Colorado, Colo. Springs | CO | Indiana University | IN |
| | | *Purdue Univ. | IN |
| Western State College | CO | Indiana State Univ. | IN |
| Gallaudet College | DC | Manchester College | IN |
| Miami Christian Col. | FL | Indiana University | IN |
| Florida International Univ. | FL | *Fort Hays State Univ. | KS |
| *University of Florida | FL | Northern Kentucky Univ. | KY |
| University of Miami | FL | Western Kentucky Univ. | KY |

| | | | |
|---|---|---|---|
| *Murray State Univ. | KY | Cameron Univ. | OK |
| *McNeese State Univ. | LA | Oklahoma City Univ. | OK |
| *Grambling State Univ. | LA | George Fox College | OR |
| *Worcester State | MA | *Oregon State Univ. | OR |
| Stone Hill College | MA | Kutztown University | PA |
| Grand Valley College | MI | *Indiana Univ. of PA | PA |
| Ferris State College | MI | Marywood College | PA |
| Bemidji State Univ. | MN | Westminster College | PA |
| Carleton College | MN | *California Univ. of PA | PA |
| St. Cloud State Univ. | MN | King's College | PA |
| Park College | MO | Millersville Univ. | PA |
| School of Ozarks | MO | Susquehanna Univ. | PA |
| Stephens College | MO | Villanova Univ. | PA |
| Avila College | MO | Wilkes College | PA |
| *University of Mo.-Columbia | MO | Rhode Island College | RI |
| University of Mo.-KC | MO | South Dakota State | SD |
| Lindenwood College | MO | David Lipscomb Col. | TN |
| Montana State Univ. | MT | *Memphis State Univ. | TN |
| Goucher College | MD | *Texas Tech. | TX |
| *Fayetteville State Univ. | NC | Trinity University | TX |
| Western Carolina Univ. | NC | Sul Ross State Univ. | TX |
| *University of NC | NC | *University of Texas | TX |
| East Carolina Univ. | NC | University of Houston | TX |
| Wayne State College | NE | *Lamar University | TX |
| Midland Lutheran Col. | NE | Sam Houston State Univ. | TX |
| Seton Hall University | NJ | Concordia Lutheran Col. | TX |
| *William Patterson Col. | NJ | Pan American Univ. | TX |
| Rider College | NJ | *North Texas State Univ. | TX |
| Eastern NM University | NM | *Wayland Baptist Univ. | TX |
| St. Francis College | NY | University of Utah | UT |
| *New School/Social Res. | NY | Virginia Western Col. | VA |
| *NY Institute of Tech. | NY | Washington & Lee Univ. | VA |
| St. Bonaventure Univ. | NY | Lyndon State Col. | VT |
| SUNY-Plattsburg | NY | Castleton State Col. | VT |
| City College | NY | Evergreen State Col. | WA |
| Kent State University | OH | Marquette University | WI |
| University of Dayton | OH | Milwaukee Area Tech. | WI |
| Cedarville College | OH | Univ. of WI-Green Bay | WI |
| *Muskingum College | OH | Univ. of WI-Oshkosh | WI |
| Xavier University | OH | *Univ. of WI-Superior | WI |
| Youngstown State Univ. | OH | Alderson-Broaddus Col. | WV |
| *Central State Univ. | OK | Marshall Univ. | WV |
| University of Tulsa | OK | | |
| Bethany Nazarene Col. | OK | | |

*Undergraduate and Graduate Programs

Graduate Program Only: Univ. of South Carolina, Columbia, SC

**Program production.** To work in program production, you will need a thorough knowledge of each element that contributes to good production values. It is important for you to have basic skills in scriptwriting, camera operation, audio and video recording and editing, graphics and special effects generation, and lighting. In a nutshell, you must be good at the craft. Concentrate on mastering the different techniques and the technologies involved in television production.

The best place to start is a basic production course at a school offering a broadcast production program. Having acquired the basics, you can develop a mastery in your area of interest through on-the-job training and workshops offered by professional associations. You may want to enhance your scriptwriting abilities by using a computer program or edit videotape using film-style techniques. You can keep abreast of developments in each production area by networking with people in the industry with similar expertise.

**Television sales.** For sales jobs, a college degree with an emphasis on advertising and marketing is preferred. An understanding of research methodology and analysis is also helpful.

**Television news.** TV jobs call for good journalistic skills such as fact-finding, data collection and analysis, interviewing, and reporting. A degree in journalism is a definite asset. Most television production jobs require practical experience with camera and other production equipment. A top-echelon television job, be it in a broadcast or corporate facility, requires five or more years of experience.

**Engineering.** Entry-level engineering and technical jobs require a high-school diploma and technical training. Top-level engineering jobs often require engineering degrees. These jobs may call for systems integration and the designing, developing, and modifying of equipment. TV engineers should be members of professional associations such as the Society of Motion Picture and Television Engineers (SMPTE), Society of Broadcast Engineers, and Society of Cable Television Engineers (SCTE). Several trade publications are good sources of information on developments in TV technologies. Among them are the *SMPTE Journal, Broadcast Engineering,* and SCTE publications.

**Administration.** Management and administrative jobs in broadcast come with extensive experience. In addition to broadcast training, these jobs call for skills in the area of business management, personnel and human resources management, finance, and broadcast law. Most management jobs call for higher education. Several publications, such as *Broadcast Management/Engineering,* provide in-depth coverage of issues and concerns relating to a broadcast manager's job. The National Association of Broadcasters (NAB) annual conference is an important industry event to attend.

**Corporate Television**       Most video managers in corporations, institutions, and governmental organizations have production skills. Most of them stay up-to-date in production techniques and technological developments by attending annual conferences held by professional associations and seminars conducted by private corporations.

The ITVA's annual conferences include roundtable discussions and workshops for managers. Expositions, seminars, and workshops such as Image World provide opportunities for video managers to improve and update management and production techniques.

To be a successful manager, you must be able to motivate your staff and have a mastery of short and long-range planning, scheduling both staff and the studio, and funding and budgeting. In addition, you must know how to select and contract outside services such as those offered by independent producers and postproduction facilities. Books and trade publications offer in-depth coverage on subjects video managers deal with on-the-job.

For a TV production job in an organization, you must be well-versed in the nuts-and-bolts of production. This includes every aspect—from conceptualization to production and distribution. You can learn basic production skills at undergraduate and graduate schools offering courses in broadcast and industrial television. Several associations provide advanced training in specific areas on state-of-the-art equipment. For example, the National Computer Graphics Association (NCGA) sponsors computer graphics tutorials, technical sessions, and an exposition annually. Those interested in interactive video should attend conferences sponsored by the Society for Advanced Learning Technologies (SALT).

Several manufacturers of professional video equipment offer training on their latest production equipment. For example, Convergence Corporation conducts workshops on editing. The Sony Institute of Applied Video Technology offers two and three-day, in-depth, hands-on workshops on a wide range of production skills.

Bear in mind that in a corporate television facility you may be called upon to do many tasks. So you must acquire proficiency in a broad range of skills. Read trade magazines regularly, as they provide articles on innovative applications areas, as well as tips on trouble-shooting. Articles on planning, production, postproduction, and distribution are covered in monthly publications such as *Video Systems, AV Video,* and *Videography.* You will find in-depth articles on ENG and film-to-tape transfers in *Millimeter* and *On-Location.*

There are very few technical jobs in corporate/organizational media departments. Some do not have on-staff TV engineers or technicians; the larger ones do. As an on-staff *TV engineer,* you will be required to plan and conduct routine maintenance procedures on all equipment. This job also calls for good negotiating skills, as you will be responsible for negotiating price and availability of equipment with vendors. You should be familiar with purchasing procedures such as RFPs (Request

For Proposals) and RFQs (Request for Quotations). You must keep abreast of new developments in television equipment.

It is necessary for television engineers and technicians to keep learning about new technologies and their uses. Associations such as the Society of Motion Picture and Television Engineers (SMPTE) and the Audio Engineering Society (AES) conduct workshops and seminars on leading-edge developments. Plan to attend the annual conferences sponsored by these associations, as well as that of the National Association of Broadcasters (NAB). You should also read trade journals and magazines such as the *SMPTE Journal, Broadcast Engineering,* and *Television Digest,* to name only a few.

### SOURCES OF INFORMATION

**Associations and Societies**

There are numerous sources to which you can write for additional information on career advancement in television, video, and film. Listed below are the names of professional associations. In Appendix A, you will find the addresses of the associations listed below.

American Society for Training and Development (ASTD)
American Video Association
American Women in Radio and Television (AWRT)
Association for Educational Communications and Technologies (AECT)
Association of Audio-Visual Technicians (AAVT)
Association of Independent TV Stations (INTV)
Association of Independent Video and Filmmakers (AIVF)
Association of Visual Communicators
(formerly Information Film Producers of America, IFPA)
Broadcast Education Association (BEA)
Cable Television Administrative and Marketing Society (CTAM)
Cable Television Advertising Bureau
Cable Television Information Center
Electronic Industries Association (EIA)
Health Education Media Association (HEMA)
Health Sciences Communications Association (HESCA)
Independent Media Producers Association, Inc. (IMPA)
International Association of Satellite Users
International Communications Industries Association (ICIA)
(formerly National Audio Visual Association NAVA)
International Interactive Communication Society (IICS)
International Radio and Television Society
International Tape/Disc Association (ITA)

International Teleconferencing Association (ITCA)
International Television Association (ITVA)
Institute of Electrical and Electronic Engineers
National Association of Broadcasters (NAB)
National Association of Television Program Executives (NATPE)
National Cable Television Association (NCTA)
National Computer Graphics Association (NCGA)
National Federation of Local Cable Programmers
National Institute for Low Power Television
National Religious Broadcasters
Radio-Television News Directors Association
Society of Broadcast Engineers
Society of Cable Television Engineers (SCTE)
Society of Motion Picture and Television Engineers (SMPTE)
Television Information Office
Videotex Industry Association
Women in Communications
Women in Cable

## PERIODICALS

Television and video publications focus coverage on different segments of the market. Some specialize in broadcast, others in organizational television, and still others in home video. Several periodicals focus on cable and teleconferencing. Periodicals listed in the chapters on film (see Chapter 4) and on multimedia (see Chapter 6) will be useful to those interested in production work. Within each of the publications listed below, you will find a good mix of news items and feature articles on the production, management, and technical aspects of the television and video industry.

Addresses appear in Appendix B.

*AV Video*
*Backstage/Backstage Shoot*
*Broadcasting & Cable*
*Broadcast Engineering*
*Cable Age*
*Cable Communications*
*Cable Marketing*
*Cable News*
*Cablevision*
*CAT Journal*
*Channels*
*Computer Pictures*
*Consumer Electronics*
*Desktop Video World*

*Millimeter*
*On-Location*
*(The) Producer's Masterguide*
*SMPTE Journal*
*Telespan Newsletter*
*Television Radio Age*
*Training*
*TV Digest*
*Variety*
*(The) Video Register (Directory)*
*Video Systems*
*Video Technology News*
*Videography*

## RECOMMENDED READING

Baldwin, Huntley. *How to Create Effective TV Commercials.* 2nd ed. Lincolnwood, IL: NTC Business Books, 1989.

Baldwin, Thomas F. and D. Stevens McVoy. *Cable Communication.* 2nd ed. Englewood Cliffs, NJ: Prentice-Hall, 1988.

Bliss, Edward Jr. and John M. Patterson. *Writing News for Broadcast.* 2nd ed. New York: Columbia University Press, 1978.

Blum, Richard A. *Television Writing.* New York: London, Woburn, MA: Focal Press, 1984.

Broughton, Irv. *The Art of Interviewing for Television, Radio and Film.* Blue Ridge Summit, PA: TAB Books, 1981.

Browne, Borz and Coddington. *Direct Broadcast Satellites: Service, Economic and Market Factors.* Washington, DC: NAB, 1981.

Brush, Judith M. and Douglas P., *Private Television Communications: The New Directions.* The Fourth Brush Report. New York: HI Press, Inc, 1986.

Burrows, Thomas D. and Donald N. Wood. *Television Production: Disciplines and Techniques.* 5th ed. Dubuque, IA: Wm. C. Brown Co., 1992.

Doyle, Marc. *The Future of Television.* Lincolnwood, IL: NTC Business Books, 1992.

Dudek, Lee J. *Professional Broadcast Announcing.* Boston: Allyn and Bacon, 1982.

Fang, Irving E. *Television News, Radio News.* 4th ed. Rada Press. St. Paul, Minn. 1985.

Gayeski, Diane M. and David V. Williams. *Interactive Media,* Prentice-Hall, Inc., New Jersey, 1985.

Hilliard, Robert L. *Writing for Television and Radio.* 5th ed. Belmont, Cal.: Wadsworth, 1991.

Howard, Herbert H. and Michael S. Kievman. *Radio and TV Programming.* Columbus, Dubuque, Iowa: Iowa State University Press, 1983.

Hyde, Stuart W. *Television and Radio Announcing.* 5th ed. Boston: Houghton Mifflin, 1986.

Leshay, Jeff. *How to Launch Your Career in TV News.* Lincolnwood, IL: *VGM Career Horizons,* 1993.

Matrazzo, Donna. *The Corporate Scriptwriting Book.* Eugene, OR: Communicom Publishing Company, 1985.

McInnes, James. *Video in Education and Training.* London, Woburn, MA: Focal Press, 1980.

Millerson, Gerald. *Effective TV Production.* 2nd ed. Boston: Focal Press, 1983.

Nash, Constance. *The Television Writer's Handbook: What to Write, How to Write it, Where to Sell it.* New York: Harper & Row, 1978.

Wurtzel, Alan. *Television Production.* 2nd ed. New York: McGraw-Hill, 1983.

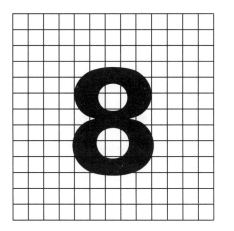

# ADVERTISING

The world of advertising is a constantly changing and exciting environment. If you have the necessary drive, ambition and competitive spirit, you should take the plunge.*

*S. William Pattis, *Opportunities in Advertising Careers* (Lincolnwood, IL: VGM Career Horizons, 1988).

Advertising is a multi-billion dollar industry, geared to a single purpose: to motivate people to "buy." Its primary communications function is persuasion. Its aim is to move people to action—to purchase a product or service, and to support a public cause or political stance. Advertising messages are paid for by the advertiser, who has control of what is said.

In a free enterprise economy, products and services abound. There is usually a greater supply of different brand products than there is a demand for that product. For instance, we have any number of options (brands) of even a basic necessity such as soap. Then there are the products and services such as home electronics and pleasure travel that compete for discretionary income.

Today, even hospitals competing for scarce patients are turning to advertising, which only a few years ago would have been dismissed as crass and unethical. Beth Israel Medical Center in New York is the first non-profit hospital in the city to advertise on television. The New Jersey Hospital Association is reportedly designing new advertising and marketing strategies for its 106 member hospitals. This is part of an effort to woo back nearly 10,000 New Jersey patients who spend more than $30 million a year in hospital care outside the state, mostly in New York City and Philadelphia.

Manufacturers and service companies alike operate in an extremely competitive marketplace. Hence, they rely on advertising to a great extent, to help sell their product. Many are increasing expenditures on advertising in support of their product marketing efforts. They use the traditional mass media—newspapers, magazines, radio, and television—to reach a greater number of people in an attempt to increase the marketshare of the product advertised. In addition, they use outdoor advertising media such as billboards, skywriting, and blimps to increase consumer awareness of their product and company. New advertising techniques such as direct mail and telemarketing are proving to be highly productive in targeting special markets.

The design and production of the advertiser's message presented through the various media requires the skills of many talented people—writers, illustrators, photographers, graphic designers, radio and television producers, to name a few. Once the advertisement has been created or produced, specialists in media selection and placement ensure that it is delivered to its target audience through the selected media. The advertising industry offers job opportunities to creative people with diverse skills, as well as to people with business acumen and training.

Several corporations have advertising departments that prepare, produce, and place company advertisements. They often utilize the services of freelance writers and graphic artists and outside media-buying companies. These companies contract the services of independent production companies to produce their radio and television commercials. Some organizations establish an in-house ad agency; others contract full-service ad agencies. People interested in advertising as a career have many avenues of work to explore.

An estimated 100,000 people work in 8,000 advertising agencies in the United States. As advertising expenditures soar, ad agencies are experiencing growth. But the annual number of agency openings for college or business school graduates is only 1,000 to 1,200 according to estimates made by the American Association of Advertising Agencies (known as the 4 As.) Hence, getting a job with an advertising agency can be highly competitive. Only about one third of the people working in advertising work for ad agencies.

### WHERE THE JOBS ARE

Each of the three parties involved in developing and executing advertising provide a job opportunity for those who have chosen advertising as a career. You can look for a job at advertising agencies, in corporate advertising departments, as well as in the media.

**Advertising Agencies**     Young creative talent and the aggressive with business savvy who want to break into advertising often think they must move to New York and "make it" on Madison Avenue. (Incidentally, many ad agencies have moved from Madison Avenue due to soaring rents on commercial space.) New York, however, continues to be the advertising capital of the world. According to *Advertising Age,* 61 of the top 100 agencies, ranked by gross income in 1985, are headquartered in New York.

You really do not have to move to New York to find a satisfying job in advertising. The U.S. Department of Commerce has a list of 8,000 existing agencies nationwide. Several New York-based agencies have well-staffed branch offices in major cities. For example, Young & Rubicam, Inc. has nearly 4,000 employees in 35 U.S. offices and some 3,000 employees in 91 foreign countries. Several large agencies are headquartered in major U.S. cities: Foote, Cone & Belding Communications in Chicago; Ketchum Communications in Pittsburgh; Campbell-Mithun in Minneapolis; Chiat/Day in Los Angeles; Tracy-Locke in Dallas; and Hill Holliday Connors Cosmopulos in Boston, to name only a few whose world gross income was over 30 million U.S. dollars in 1985.

You can start your career and gain experience in a large agency environment by working at their offices in any major city. Large agencies generally have a broad range of clients and therefore can provide you with a variety of work. You can also start your career with a small agency in the city of your choice and specialize in a particular type of advertising or client.

The *Standard Directory of Advertising Agencies,* known as the *Agency Red Book,* is an excellent research tool when you are looking for an agency job. It lists over 4,000 agencies and includes regional offices, accounts, specialization, number of employees, and the names and titles of key personnel. The *Agency Red Book* is published every February, June, and October.

## Corporate Advertising Departments

Many large corporations (and nearly every very large one) have advertising departments. Since corporations are clients of ad agencies and in fact the advertisers, corporate ad departments are often referred to as "client departments." It is the function of such a department either to act as liaison between the company and the company's ad agency or to produce the company's advertising and sales promotion material.

As liaison, a corporate ad department is responsible for establishing advertising goals and ensuring that the advertising prepared by their agency fits the company's sales and marketing objectives. Since this department is held responsible for the agency's performance, it is usually vested with the authority to approve or disapprove the agency's recommendations. In a very large corporation for example, if the ad department is headed by a vice president, the decision to hire or fire an agency can be made at the department level. Depending on the size of the corporate ad department and the title of its highest executive, however, final approval may have to come from a higher level of management.

In some corporations, the advertising department is responsible for creating and producing advertising and sales materials including catalogs, brochures, and other collateral material. For instance, a major retail or department store such as Bloomingdale's or Macy's will maintain a large creative staff and ad department to handle daily ads and the continuous flow of new catalogs. Corporate departments responsible for the preparation and placement of materials are staffed in much the same way as ad agencies. They hire *researchers, copywriters, visualizers, graphic artists, creative directors, advertising assistants,* and *ad managers.*

The *Standard Directory of Advertisers,* referred to as the *Advertiser Red Book,* lists more than 17,000 advertisers (organizations) including budgets, advertising agency, and the names and titles of key personnel. If you are interested in a job with a corporate advertising department, the *Advertiser Red Book* will prove to be a good resource.

**The Media**

Every newspaper, magazine, radio, and television station employs an advertising staff. Media advertising jobs are primarily sales. Advertising sales staff sell ad space for their publications or time for their radio or TV station to agencies and advertisers. For job-seekers not interested in selling, there are also some sales support and creative jobs available, especially in large media companies such as CBS or Murdoch Magazines. Sales support functions include market research and the production of collateral materials, as well as some ad materials.

An *advertising sales manager* or *advertising sales director* is usually in charge of a media ad sales department. *Creative directors* or *art directors* are generally responsible for the creative services staff. Large media conglomerates have research departments headed by a *research director.*

If you are interested in an advertising sales job with the media, you should check *Folio:400* for a magazine sales position. *Folio* does an analysis and media ranking of consumer and trade publications. Also check the *Ayer Directory of Publications* and *Standard Rate & Data Service* (SRDS.) For sales jobs with radio and television stations, use *Broadcasting Yearbook*. If you are interested in the creative aspects of advertising, your best resource is professional associations such as the Society of Illustrators. This association publishes *Society of Illustrators' Career Guidance in Illustration and Graphics Design,* a booklet that discusses portfolio preparation, gives detailed job descriptions of agency jobs, and hints on how to get in to see an art director. The One Club for copywriters and art directors also offers career guidance and a job placement service.

## THE JOBS

Most ad agencies are organized into the following departments: administration or agency management, account management, creative services, media services, print production, traffic, finance and bookkeeping. Large and medium-sized agencies may have specialists in each department, as well as a separate department for research, television production, and human resources (personnel.)

**Administration**

Although agency management is always a critical function, the trend toward mega-agencies is making it more so. The management function includes responsibility for establishing policies, as well as planning, developing, and defining objectives to assure growth and profitability. At small agencies, this function is carried out by the *owner, president,* or *partners.* A super-large agency may be managed by a *chief executive officer* (CEO), *chief operating officer* (COO), and *chief financial officer* (CFO) with an executive committee or board of directors, in much the same way as a large corporation.

**Account Management**

The function of this department is to write the market plan, present the plan and get it approved by the client, coordinate the development of the advertising program, and ensure that the approved program is implemented. These functions are executed by an account group consisting of a *management supervisor, account supervisor, account executive, account coordinator,* and *account assistant.* In a small agency, the account group may consist of fewer people, each carrying greater responsibilities.

An account group acts as liaison between agency and client. Every member of this group has a counterpart on the client side—the higher up the account person, the higher up her or his client contact. For example, a management supervisor will interact with the vice president of marketing, the account supervisor with the director of sales and advertising, and the account executive with the advertising manager.

**Creative Services**

The creative department is where an ad is conceptualized and created. The creative team consisting of *art directors, copywriters, graphic artists, illustrators, photographers, TV producers,* and *layout* and *mechanical artists* all work together to translate market strategy into advertising—print ads and commercials for broadcast. This group is also responsible for the production of collateral materials such as logos and displays.

The function of the art department varies from agency to agency depending on the number of clients, billings, and the type of work required by the art department. For example, if the service offered by an agency includes production of commercials, the art department will be responsible for conceptualizing split-media ads. Once the department has come up with an idea and plan that is "on target," it is presented to the client for approval. The department is then responsible for the production of the ad.

The *art director* works with writers and the creative team to conceive and develop imaginative and persuasive print and television advertisements. The art director has to prepare cost estimates relating to layout, illustration, photography, type, retouching, and pasteup. This job involves the supervision of all staff involved in producing the various elements that make the ad.

Entry into the creative department of an ad agency is extremely competitive. For a job in this department, you must be able to present your portfolio to the art director. This in itself is a very tough job. However, most creative departments utilize the services of *freelance writers, photographers,* and *graphic artists.* One way to gain entry for employment in this department is by presenting your portfolio as a freelancer.

## Media Services

The function of this department is to analyze, evaluate, select, and recommend the appropriate media for the client's ads. The newspapers, magazines, radio, and television stations selected must be best suited to meet the objectives of the advertising strategy.

Job titles in this department include *media director, media supervisor, broadcast media supervisor, media planner, media buyer,* and *media estimator.*

The key responsibility of the *media director* is to set internal policies on media planning and buying. Since this is a senior position, the job calls for maintaining good relations with the media, as well as developing new profit opportunities. *Media supervisors* develop and execute media plans that will meet clients' advertising objectives. They have to make formal presentations to both the agency's account group, as well as the client. Media supervisors guide the work of media planners.

Large agencies hire *broadcast media supervisors* to analyze and evaluate broadcast media, develop demographics and cost estimates, and negotiate radio and television buys. The main task of the *media planner* is to work up and traffic media schedules. Developing a media schedule entails media research, the selection of a combination of media with advertising schedules.

*Media buyers* are responsible for negotiating and purchasing space and time. As most publications have virtually unlimited space for sale, buying magazine space calls for the ability to negotiate position (i.e., getting the best position in the magazine for your client's ad). In radio and television, buyers are given the specifications against which to find the best spots for the advertiser's purposes. Media buyers have to find out what spots are available before negotiating a purchase. Since rates for spots are flexible, the purchase of broadcast spots (known as "avails," since they depend on availability) requires skill and experience.

Some large companies hire entry-level people as *media estimators.* The job involves compiling rates/cost data for media buyers and planners. This is a good entry-level position because it is accompanied by on-the-job training necessary to become a media buyer.

## Print Production

The print production department is responsible for the final creation of the advertisement. After the creative team has finalized and specified the various elements of the ad, the print production people purchase elements such as color separations and type. Print production managers are responsible for black-and-white and four-color printing, color separations, and the preparation of mechanicals.

This department works closely with the traffic and creative departments in scheduling and coordinating production projects. It is also responsible for quality control of the final advertising materials, to ensure that they are technically correct and on time. Entry into this department is not highly competitive, though it usually calls for some experience in production work. An entry-level position in this department is the best stepping-stone to higher responsibilities and better-paying jobs in the agency.

**Traffic**

Managers, supervisors, and assistants in the traffic department control and oversee the flow of work to ensure that ads are conceived, produced, and placed as specified. Hence this department's primary function is to establish schedules and serve as mediator between production staff, creative, and account groups. This group is also responsible for complete recordkeeping from the account group's "job order" to completion. A *traffic assistant's* position requires little experience and therefore is an excellent entry-level job. It requires basic organizational skills.

**Finance and Bookkeeping**

Specialists in accounting, financing, and financial forecasting are hired by ad agencies to monitor all financial transactions. This includes collecting money from clients, paying the media and other creditors, and meeting payroll payments. Agencies gain frequency discounts from the media when making multiple-unit buys; however, the agency must pay that media within a given period of time. Since most clients rarely pay the agency in advance, leaving the agency to lay out huge sums of money in the interim, a critical function of this department is managing cash flow.

## EDUCATION AND EXPERIENCE

**Education.**   Most major universities, colleges, and professional schools offer courses in the various aspects of advertising. For example, you can study writing, photography, broadcast, and public relations techniques as part of a communications program. Courses in graphic design, lettering, typography, pasteup and mechanical preparation, and illustration are usually offered by schools of art. Courses in advertising, marketing, and magazine advertising sales are taught at business schools.

Advertising-related courses can be taken as part of a degree program or as noncredit courses. Seminars and workshops are also offered by professional societies and schools of continuing education. Those interested in programs at the college level should check Texas Tech University's booklet entitled "Where Shall I Go to Study Advertising?". A selected list of colleges offering courses in advertising is presented later in this chapter.

A prerequisite to entry in advertising is a good foundation in written and oral communication skills supported by a high-school degree. Because the marketplace is highly competitive, college education in advertising, marketing, or journalism is becoming more and more of a necessity to enter advertising. There are, however, some jobs in production and traffic that do not require a college degree.

**Experience.**   Agency management positions are granted to people with several years of broad experience in advertising. Typically, top management jobs are acquired after considerable managerial experience in a high-level position. The title of *account management supervisor* is granted as promotion to a person with several years of experience as an *account supervisor.* This position exists in large agencies. An account supervisor must have two to five years of experience as an account executive. *Account executives* generally join a firm as *assistant account executives* with some management training. An MBA is preferred.

*Creative directors* and *senior art directors* are expected to have six to eight years of experience with much of it in the area of art direction. Senior art directors must have three to five years of experience as an art director or as assistant art director.

A top-level *copywriter's* job at a large agency would require that you have from three to eight years of copywriting experience. This job requires experience at managing a full team of writers. Some agencies hire *junior copywriters* without extensive experience, if their portfolios look promising.

A media director's job calls for more than five years of experience, in addition to several years of work in the business. This job can lead to an agency management position, depending on the size of the agency and its organizational structure. The title of *media supervisor* is granted to those with two or three years of experience as *media planners* or *buyers.*

A *traffic manager* must have at least three to five years of experience specifically in traffic.

Most management titles at large and medium-sized agencies call for experience in supervising and managing a department.

**Account management.**   The jobs of account executives and account supervisors require a thorough understanding of the advertising industry and a good business sense. A liberal arts education with broad experience is helpful in handling clients of diverse backgrounds. You must have well-developed interpersonal skills and be self confident and flexible. Agencies look for good business communicators with management qualifications. If you are planning on higher education, an MBA would be appropriate. Professional associations such as the Ad Club of New York and the American Management Association offer a wide variety of noncredit courses on advertising and marketing.

**Creative services.**    To get a job in this area, you must have exceptional talent. Writers, illustrators, and photographers working in this department are specialists in their specific creative fields. In addition, each must understand the advertising business. For example, a copywriter, in addition to writing imaginative and stimulating copy, must have a sense of design. As a creative person, you must be able to express your ideas in the context of the marketplace. You must know the client's product, its users, and its competition. You must have a good understanding of the media in which the advertising message will be presented. In addition, you must have a clear understanding of the marketing plan and advertising strategy.

Ad agencies seek out outstanding graphic designers. It is the visual element of an ad that grabs the reader or viewer. If you are interested in the design aspects of advertising, you must know about different typefaces and sizes, and how to arrange type and illustration in an uncluttered and eye-catching manner. As an art director, you will not actually have to draw the final graphic element in the ad (this is handled by the print production people), but you will need to sketch the idea, to demonstrate to the client how the finished ad will look. Hence, training in an art or design school is essential. Courses in the various aspects of design are offered in art schools such as the School of Visual Arts and Parsons/ New School for Social Research in New York. Creative people should study publications of The Clio Organization, sponsor of CLIO, the Award for Advertising Excellence.

**Print production.**    Whatever your title in the print production department, you are expected to have a broad knowledge of all areas of graphic arts and have a critical eye for color. As a print production manager, you must be well versed in scheduling and monitoring production jobs. You must be familiar with vendors such as printers, typographers, engravers, and retouchers. You must also know the strengths and weaknesses of each supplier. As you will be responsible for production budget control, you must understand the cost-efficiencies in terms of time and quality, in getting the job done.

**Traffic.**    Scheduling and coordination of people and projects are essential skills required of people working in the traffic department. You must have an eye for detail, be well organized, and have the ability to handle several tasks simultaneously. You will have to interface with the creative, print production, and account groups, so you must have a pleasant personality and the ability to nudge people on, to ensure work flow. As a senior person in this department, you will be responsible for preparing preliminary budgets and securing internal, as well as client and legal, approvals.

## COLLEGE ADVERTISING COURSES

A selected list of colleges offering courses in advertising is presented below. Every effort has been made to make this a comprehensive list, but as changes can occur rapidly, you should also check with local and state schools and with the American Advertising Federation for any additional choices at the time you wish to choose a school.

In addition to colleges offering advertising courses, many other schools have courses in marketing, journalism, design, and other advertising-related courses which you will also want to investigate.

Arizona State University
Ball State University
Boston University
Bowling Green State University
Brigham Young University
California State
   University–Fresno
California State
   University–Fullerton
Central State University
City University of New York
College of New Rochelle
Columbia College
Creighton University
DePaul University
Drake University
Ferris State College
Florida State University
Indiana University
Iowa State University
Kansas State University
Kent State University
Louisiana State University
Marquette University
Marshall University
Memphis State University
Michigan State University
Middle Tennessee State University
Moorehead State University
Murray State University
New Mexico State University
New York University
North Texas State University
Northern Arizona University
Northern Illinois University
Northwestern University

Ohio University
Oklahoma State University
Pennsylvania State University
Roosevelt University
San Jose State University
South Dakota State University
Southern Illinois University
Southern Methodist University
Southwest Texas State University
Syracuse University
Temple University
Texas Christian University
Texas Tech University
University of Alabama
University of Arkansas–Little
   Rock
University of Bridgeport
University of Central Florida
University of Colorado
University of Dayton
University of Florida
University of Georgia
University of Illinois
University of Kansas
University of Kentucky
University of Maine
University of Maryland
University of Minnesota
University of Mississippi
University of Missouri
University of Nebraska
University of Nevada–Reno
University of North
   Carolina–Chapel Hill
University of North Dakota
University of Oklahoma

University of Oregon
University of Rhode Island
University of South Carolina
University of South Florida
University of Southern
  Mississippi
University of Tennessee-Knoxville
University of Texas-Austin
University of Washington
University of Wisconsin-Eau
  Claire
University of Wisconsin-Madison
University of Wisconsin-Oshkosh
University of Wyoming
Virginia Commonwealth
  University
Washington State University
West Virginia University
Western Kentucky University
Western Michigan University
Wichita State University
Youngstown State University

## SOURCES OF INFORMATION

**Associations and Societies**

The professional organizations listed here can assist you in learning more about a particular area of advertising. Many of them publish pamphlets, periodicals, and books that can help in your career advancement. Addresses appear in Appendix A.

The Advertising Club of New York
The Advertising Council
Advertising Research Foundation
Advertising Women of New York
American Advertising Federation
American Association of Advertising Agencies (known as the 4 A's)
American Institute of Graphic Arts
American Marketing Association
Art Directors Club of New York
Association of National Advertisers
Business/Professional Advertising Association
Cabletelevision Advertising Bureau, Inc.
Council of Sales Promotion Agencies
Direct Mail Marketing Association
Institute of Outdoor Advertising
Magazine Publishers Association
National Advertising Review Board
Newspaper Advertising Bureau
National Association of Publisher Representatives
The One Club
Outdoor Advertising Association of America
Point of Purchase Advertising Institute
Premium Advertising Association of America

Print Advertising Association
Promotional Marketing Association of America
Radio Advertising Bureau
Society of Illustrators
Specialty Advertising Association International
Specialty Advertising Information Bureau
Television Bureau of Advertising
The Transit Advertising Association, Inc.

## PERIODICALS AND DIRECTORIES

There are numerous newsletters, magazines, and directories published
for advertising professionals. The list presented here is a selection for
those working in different departments of an agency or corporate ad departments. Several publications not listed here provide specific information on advertising in special markets such as health and incentives
groups. People working or seeking work in public relations divisions of
ad agencies should read Chapter 9 of this book. If you are interested in
broadcast advertising, check the publications list in Chapters 5 and 7.
The creative group should refer to the publications recommended in
Chapters 2 and 6.

*Ad East*
*Ad Forum*
*Advertising Age*
*Advertising and Communications Yellow Pages*
*Advertising/Communications Times*
*Advertising World*
*Adweek*
*American Newspaper Markets Circulation*
*Art Direction*
*Art Product News*
*Broadcasting Yearbook*
*Briefings*
*Business Marketing*
*Communication Arts*
*Creative: The Magazine of Promotion and Marketing*
*The Creative Black Book*
*Dartnell Sales and Marketing Service*
*Direct Marketing*
*The Direct Marketing Market Place*
*DM News, The Newspaper of Direct Marketing*

*The Folio:400*
*The Gallagher Report*
*Graphic Design:USA*
*International Advertiser*
*Journal of Marketing*
*Madison Avenue*
*Magazine Age*
*Marketing and Media Decisions*
*Marketing Communications*
*Potentials in Marketing*
*Print: America's Graphic Design Magazine*
*Signs of the Times*
*Specialty Advertising Business*
*Standard Directory of Advertisers*
*Standard Directory of Advertising Agencies (Agency Red Book)*
*Standard Rate & Data Service*
*Zip/Target Marketing*

## RECOMMENDED READING

Barban, Arnold M. et al. *Advertising Media Sourcebook*. 3rd ed. Lincolnwood, IL: NTC Business Books, 1989.

Bogart, Leo. *Strategy in Advertising: Matching Media and Messages to Markets and Motivations*. 2nd ed. Lincolnwood, IL: NTC Business Books, 1984.

Bovee, Courtland L. and William F. Arens. *Contemporary Advertising*. 4th ed. Homewood, IL: Richard D. Irwin, Inc., 1992.

Evans, Joel R. and Barry Berman. *Marketing*. 3rd ed. New York: Macmillan Publishing Company, 1987.

Ganim, Barbara. *How to Approach an Advertising Agency and Walk Away With the Job You Want*. Lincolnwood, IL: VGM Career Horizons, 1993.

Gibson, Arthur, et al. *Truth in Advertising*. N.P.: E. Mellen, 1982.

Minski, Laurence and Emily Thomton Calvo. *How to Succeed in Advertising When All You Have Is Talent*. Lincolnwood, IL: NTC Business Books, 1994.

Paetro, Maxine. *How To Put Your Book Together and Get a Job in Advertising*. New York: Chicago, IL: The Copy Workshop, 1991.

Stone, Bob. *Successful Direct Marketing Methods*. 5th ed. Lincolnwood, IL: NTC Business Books, 1994.

Watkins, Julian L. *The One Hundred Greatest Advertisements: Who Wrote Them and What They Did*. 2nd ed. New York: Dover, 1959.

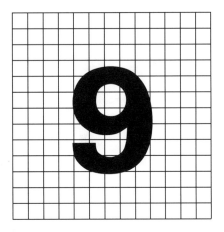

# PUBLIC RELATIONS

The entire nation—even the world—is the environment of the public relations practitioner. Information is his tool. Communications is his strategy. Persuasion is his objective.*

---

*Tony De Lorenzo

Public relations is the means by which an organization presents itself to the public. It is an action program designed to build and maintain a positive image of the organization. Hence, it focuses on the attitudes and concerns of the organization's designated publics: its customers, employees, and stockholders. The primary responsibility of a PR practitioner is to develop a two-way communications channel between an organization and its specific audience. The message in this communications process includes everything that is vital to the daily functioning of the organization. The information may be how-to or marketing-oriented; motivational or judgmental; controversial, disaster-related, or good news (such as profits and promotions).

Traditionally, public relations was conducted primarily for the purpose of influencing or persuading an audience to think favorably of an organization. Public relations practitioners were often derogatorily labeled propagandists. Some of them concentrated only on presentation skills and often engaged in less than complimentary methods of influencing the press, thereby gaining a favorable position for the organization they represented.

Today, however, the profession commands greater stature and importance. Over the past decade and a half, public relations has developed into a science and an art, thanks to the experience and dedication of scholars and specialists. They have urged practitioners to focus on the substance of their message, as well as on the presentation of it. They have insisted on the formal training of would-be practitioners. Their trade association, The Public Relations Society of America (PRSA), has as its main objective the task of developing and promoting high standards of public service and conduct among its members. Toward that end, the society developed and adopted a code of professional standards that emphasizes a practitioner's ethical responsibility.

Profit and nonprofit organizations in both the private and public sectors are finding it increasingly difficult to communicate effectively with their key audiences. One reason is information overload. More corporations are giving out more information than ever before. In an age of information proliferation, the responsibility of public relations staffs to disseminate information, handle conflict and controversy, and build the company image has become more critical. In this age of rapid social change and shifting values, institutions are relying on public relations specialists to help establish sound relationships with various publics. They realize that public understanding and support are factors critical to achieving organizational goals.

Corporations and institutions are striving to understand the forces of change and are constantly adapting their activities to new aspirations. As they lean on public relations practitioners to help win public support and trust, the PR profession is gaining respect and prominence. The profession has come a long way from the time when practitioners were called propagandists, to being referred to as counselors today. Public relations practitioners are interpreters of management's policies, programs, and practices to the public, and are translators of the public's attitude toward management.

In recent times, several corporations have experienced public image crisis situations. Incidents like the deaths from tampered-with medicine capsules damage the reputation of a company instantly and require an immediate and tactful PR effort. During any emergency, it is essential that the news media, employees, and the public at large be handled in an intelligent and forthright manner.

The U.S. Bureau of Labor statistics indicate that there are 143,000 people working in public relations jobs nationwide. They work in various types of companies and institutions, including banks, hospitals, religious organizations, public utilities, labor unions, and colleges and universities, to name a few.

## WHERE THE JOBS ARE

The field of public relations has a wide range of practice. Nearly every segment of society can use the service of a public relations specialist to promote an idea or help sell a product. The opportunity to perform public relations functions exists in every organization that needs to address a defined public. For example, a hospital would need to make the community aware of healthcare issues and the services it provides. Similarly, a hotel would need to inform the travel and tourism industry of its new facilities and services. Many businesses, associations, and government departments have job opportunities for PR practitioners. In addition, firms that provide public relations services for corporations hire trained PR people.

**Public Relations Firms**

PR firms, like advertising agencies, handle accounts from different companies. There are over 4,000 PR firms nationwide. New York and Chicago are the largest metropolitan centers with heavy concentrations of public relations firms or counselors. PR firms vary in size depending on the number of clients they have and the size of the clients' budgets. They range in staff size from one-person consultants, to a few PR generalists hired at small agencies, to more than a hundred employed at larger firms. Most firms carry varied accounts, but some specialize in industrial or consumer marketing programs, financial or investor relations, government relations, and employee communications. PR job descriptions vary from agency to agency. For example, in a small agency you may have the title of accounts supervisor but may be called upon to do the job of an account executive and at times, even that of an accounts writer. If you are seeking a job with a public relations firm, you should consult the *O'Dwyer's Directory of Public Relations Firms/O'Dwyer's Profiles: 25 Largest PR Operations.*

**Advertising Agencies**

Large advertising agencies have PR departments or own public relations subsidiaries to service their major clients. For example, the J. Walter Thompson Group, one of the largest worldwide advertising agencies, owns Hill and Knowlton, which is a major PR firm.

**Government**

The United States government is perhaps the single largest employer of press secretaries, information officers, public affairs experts, and communications specialists. The task of these individuals, who work out of national, state, regional, county, and district offices is to communicate the activities of the various agencies, bureaus, and commissions to the public.

The International Communications Agency (ICA) is perhaps the most far-reaching public communications arm of the United States federal government. It employs nearly 9,000 people and has a worldwide network encompassing 100 countries.

Many renowned public relations consultants started in the field as public information officers (PIOs) for the nation's military. The army, navy, air force, and marines employ people in this capacity. The military offers in-service communications training. The Defense Information School is located at Fort Benjamin Harrison, Indianapolis. The U.S. Department of Defense has a public affairs budget of $23 million.

The U.S. Department of Health, Education, and Welfare had a public affairs staff of nearly 1,000 people and a budget of approximately $23 million. The U.S. Department of Agriculture too has a large communications staff.

**Corporations**

The economic wheels of business and industry generate the funds necessary to meet public relations budgets of billions of dollars annually. Almost every corporation has a department of communications from which PR functions are carried out. The purpose of the PR function is to maintain employee relations in-house, as well as to promote the company's product and services externally.

In a corporation, the PR task will vary according to the size of the company and the type of industry. In a public utility company, the job will be geared to developing good customer and government relations. In an industrial or consumer company, the PR job would involve developing strategies to promote the product and the corporate image.

**Nonprofit Institutions**

The public relations function in nonprofit organizations such as the American Red Cross is primarily directed toward fundraising activities. There are over 14,000 national associations, the majority of which are headquartered in Washington, DC; New York, or Chicago. The main PR function of an association is to create a favorable climate for an industry or cause.

Information bureaus, institutions, councils, and foundations also engage in PR activities relating to matters of public concern such as environmental protection, safety, and nutrition. Voluntary agencies in the health and public service sector provide varied job opportunities in press, community, and patron relations, as well as in fundraising.

### THE JOBS

**Public Relations Firms**

Within a public relations firm or the PR department of an advertising agency, public relations practitioners typically carry the general job titles and functions described below. However, you must keep in mind that PR job descriptions vary from firm to firm, depending on the size of firm and types of clients. Large PR firms often hire account executives with special expertise such as investor relations.

**Public relations director.** *Public relations director* or *director of PR services* at an advertising agency is a top-level job requiring management experience and extensive knowledge of advertising and PR techniques. This person has full responsibility for setting objectives and overseeing projects, establishing policies and budgets, and setting fees for accounts. The job also calls for maintaining contact with clients.

**Account supervisor.** The *account supervisor* is the primary link between an individual client and the agency, and performs a managerial role, integrating PR plans with the client's marketing effort. Many PR firms also have a need for account supervisors with specialized expertise in particular industries (for example, theatrical, financial, and community relations).

**Account executive.** The *account executive* participates in developing PR plans and is specifically responsible for implementing them. Since this is basically a "doing function," it is essential for an account executive to be a good coordinator. The job involves contact with the press, to gain adequate editorial coverage. Training or experience in journalism or public relations would prove a plus for this job.

**Account writer.** The *account writer's* main task is research and writing. The PR writer's assignments include writing press releases, speeches, reports, and product information.

**PR researcher.** The PR researcher's job involves information gathering and fact finding in order to prepare speeches and news releases. It also involves opinion research and audience surveys which provide data used in the designing of PR programs.

**Production supervisor.** Large PR firms hire production supervisors to handle assignments for printing, graphics, and other production work. It is necessary for a production supervisor to maintain production records on all PR accounts.

**PR assistant.** This job provides a good mix of all functions basic to PR. It is therefore a good position for launching into a PR career. Daily tasks include follow-up on production schedules, research, some writing, coordination of special events, and maintaining records. The job is a basic support service to all PR personnel.

**Government.** Bureaus, commissions, and departments of government employ public information officers to disseminate information on their policies and activities.

**Corporate Public Relations**

In a corporation, the public relations staff may be located in the public affairs, communications, or media department. It is often part of the marketing and advertising department. In smaller companies, all PR functions are carried out by one person. Large PR departments have a person responsible for each function. The director of public relations is in charge of the PR staff.

The main purpose of corporate PR activity is to gain publicity, promote a product or service, develop community relations, and maintain government relations. The publicity task calls for the planning and development of a campaign which involves the selection of information to be disseminated and the media to be used. The most important and frequently used tools are press releases, feature articles, news letters, press conferences, press kits, and interviews between corporate management and reporters.

Speech writing is regarded as a coveted function within corporate public relations departments as it wins the writer recognition from top management. Public relations promotion activities provide an added force to advertising, sales, and marketing programs. Promotion experts are required to be highly creative as they are called upon to conceive, develop, and execute unique and novel methods of influencing consumers.

**Community relations.**  Most corporations seek to achieve community acceptance by highlighting their contribution to the welfare of the community. To achieve this, the PR job calls for recommending sponsorship of special cause-related events such as the concert Live Aid for Africa. It could also include sponsorship of cultural shows such as Mobile Corporation's sponsorship of Masterpiece Theater on public television.

**Government relations.**  PR people who handle government relations strive to improve communications with government personnel and agencies, to monitor legislators and regulatory agencies and, most important, to influence legislation affecting the company and the industry at large. Public relations practitioners in the field of government relations must understand the federal government setup, have access to government communications channels, and maintain contacts with government staff.

**Nonprofit institutions.**  Public relations for most nonprofit organizations such as churches and hospitals primarily involves fundraising activities. Fundraisers must be good letterwriters, brochure writers, and public speakers. They must have full knowledge of the sources and procedures for obtaining monies from foundations and government grants.

## EDUCATION

A public relations specialist must have knowledge and skills in a wide range of areas, including journalism, speech, and communications techniques, as well as political science, sociology, and psychology. Top-level jobs require managerial experience and often training in economics, finance, and business administration. Writing, counseling, and judgment make up the backbone of all PR functions.

A liberal arts background is arguably the best undergraduate preparation for a public relations career. Some experts argue that writing and communication skills are important for entry into the field and that graduate studies in finance, marketing, and business administration are necessary to ascend the career ladder.

Anyone considering a career as a publicist or a public relations specialist must be a people person. Public relations is a function of the process of persuasion. Hence prerequisites to entry in the field are strong interpersonal skills and the innate ability to sell.

**Writing.** The primary task of all PR responsibilities is writing. Therefore you must develop the ability to write easily, clearly, concisely, coherently, and quickly. The most essential writing skill is versatility in style. While a good news style is necessary for writing a press release, you must also be able to write feature articles and case histories for magazines. Likewise, you must know the difference between writing for the eye and writing for the ear. When writing a speech for example, you should write an introduction that will grab the audience and hold its interest. A business style is necessary when writing a white paper, a proposal, or an annual report.

Not everyone is born a writer. But most people can be trained to write. Good writing, like any other skill, can only get better with practice. Once you have mastered the fundamentals of writing, the more you write, the better you will get at it. Practice also builds writing speed, which is vital in a fast-paced PR environment. Typing and word processing skills are essential supplementary tools of the trade.

The importance of editing in breathing life into dull copy can hardly be overstated. Well-honed editing skills will ensure that all of your written material has the desired impact.

Journalism and communications schools teach writing and editing. A journalism or communications degree is a good entry into the field of public relations.

**Research.** Informal research is used on a daily basis by PR practitioners. Formal, qualitative, and quantitative research is conducted less frequently. Informal interviews and opinion surveys are often used in the preparation of speeches, press releases, and proposals. Formal, analytical research is usually conducted with specific objectives, such as determining the basic attitudes or awareness levels of certain audiences or test marketing campaign themes. In the public relations environment, the most widely used methodologies are fact-finding research, attitudinal studies, and opinion surveys.

Library and survey research skills are considered a plus for entry-level job candidates. A basic undergraduate course on social research or research methods is all you need. However, it is becoming increasingly important for advanced professionals to be familiar with current research methodologies and be able to interpret statistical information.

In the 19th Foundation lecture, delivered at the 1980 convention of the Public Relations Society of America, Scott Jones, senior consultant for Hill and Knowlton, emphasized that PR executives must get into "futures research." He was referring to a technique the experts call future scanning, which is rapidly emerging as a prerequisite for strategic planning. The August 1980 issue of the *Financier* published an article entitled "The Future Can Be Researched" by Robert L. Thaler and Hank E. Koehn. The authors say that futures research involves a continual monitoring of the world for those bits of information that indicate something different is happening.

In futures research, you scan newspapers, magazines, polls, reports, and studies for items that might ordinarily escape notice—items that are indicators of future direction. The process reveals information about the competition and consumer acceptance of new products and services. This research method, it is believed, will indicate areas of need not yet being serviced. Futures research is expected to be the drawing board upon which societal patterns of behavior or trends will emerge.

Jones urges public relations professionals who aspire to reach policy-making levels in their organizations to get involved in futures research. It will equip you to be an "early warning system" for your employer, which in turn will lead to greater upward mobility for you, professionally.

**Oral communications skills.** As spokespeople for the organizations they represent, PR people must have the ability to address audiences and present information in an honest, straightforward, and interesting manner. Most important is the ability to communicate financial and technical information in a clear and comprehensible fashion. As a spokesperson, you are expected to be articulate and thoroughly knowledgeable on the subject you are presenting. Handling questions and controlling an audience are equally important skills. Training in public speaking can help enhance oral and presentation skills.

**Management.** Time and people management are perhaps the most essential skills required by a public relations practitioner with supervisory responsibilities. In addition, senior-level public relations professionals must be good at financial planning and budgeting. In a corporate environment, knowledge of legal and financial affairs will undoubtedly make for upward mobility on the career ladder.

You must start developing time and people management skills with your first step in the PR field. In this high-pressure environment, you must consciously manage your time and your clients' time carefully. You will find yourself constantly juggling and coordinating schedules and budgets. You must be able to do so with sensitivity to the people involved in the project. While effectively managing time and people on a project-to-project basis, you must continue to maintain good interpersonal relationships with all your clients and your staff.

If you want to make it to the top, you must acquire business and administrative skills. You will need them if you plan to work with an agency and more so if you are in corporate communications. Your need for finance and business skills will be greatest if you launch out on your own and start a PR firm. The place to learn good management skills and practices is a business school. There are many publications—books and magazines on management. Read them. Trade associations such as the American Management Association conduct workshops on each aspect of management. Attend them. If your goal is an upper-level corporate position, your chances will be best if you have an MBA. So start working toward it right now.

## ACCREDITED COLLEGES AND UNIVERSITIES

The public relations sequences of the following colleges and universities have been accredited by the Public Relations Society of America (PRSA). A joint commission, composed of members of the Accrediting Council on Education in Journalism and Mass Communications (ACEJMC) and the Public Relations Society of America, accredits public relations sequences in schools of journalism.

Schools offering master's degrees in journalism and mass communications are indicated with one asterisk (*); schools offering doctoral degrees are indicated with two asterisks (**).

*Ball State University, Department of Journalism

Bowling Green State University, School of Journalism

Brigham Young University, Department of Communications

California State University–Fresno, Department of Journalism

California State University–Fullerton, Department of Journalism

Colorado State University, Department of Technical Journalism

*Drake University, School of Journalism and Mass Communication

Florida A&M University, School of Journalism, Media, and Graphic Arts

*Kansas State University, Department of Journalism and Mass Communication

Kent State University, School of Journalism

*Marshall University, W. Page Pitt School of Journalism

Memphis State University, Department of Journalism

*Northern Illinois University, Department of Journalism

**Ohio University, E.W. Scripps School of Journalism

*Ohio State University, School of Journalism

*Oklahoma State University, School of Journalism and Broadcasting

St. Cloud State University, Department of Mass Communications

*San Diego State University, Department of Journalism

*San Jose State University, Department of Journalism and Mass Communications

\*\*Syracuse University, S. I. Newhouse School of Public Communications

Temple University, Department of Journalism

\*\*Texas Tech University, Department of Mass Communications

University of Alabama, School of Communication

University of Florida, College of Journalism and Communications

\*University of Georgia, Henry W. Grady School of Journalism and Mass Communication

\*\*University of Maryland, College of Journalism

\*University of Oklahoma, H.H. Hebert School of Journalism and Mass Communication

\*University of Oregon, School of Journalism

University of South Florida, Department of Mass Communications

University of Southern California, School of Journalism

\*\*University of Tennessee–Knoxville, College of Communications

\*\*University of Texas–Austin, College of Communication

\*\*West Virginia University, Perley Isaac Reed School of Journalism

## PERSONAL CHARACTERISTICS

In order to achieve excellence and be truly outstanding in this highly competitive and visible field, you must, at the very outset, master the basic skill—communications. The next important ingredient is a thorough knowledge of the business or field in which your organization operates. If your company is in the travel industry, it is imperative that you keep abreast of developments in that field. Leadership qualities and management techniques will help you broaden the dimensions of your job and achieve the highest levels of professional excellence. In addition to all of that, the following personal characteristics must be continuously nurtured for a successful career.

**Intellect.** A keen intellect is necessary to identify a problem and provide a solution immediately. In today's environment of accelerated social change, it is important for PR people to keep up-to-date on all issues. They must read everything they can and keep learning constantly.

**Integrity.** Truth and credibility are the cornerstones of good public relations. PR professionals must have the highest level of integrity and be able to command credibility on behalf of the organizations they represent. Pressure from government agencies and advocate groups obligates organizations to tell the truth in areas such as product labeling and financial reporting. PR professionals must have the courage of their conviction to let clients or employers know when they are in the wrong.

**Perspective.** In order to be able to project a positive image of a company, you need to view the total activities of the company in the larger social, political, and business context. In addition, a practitioner needs to maintain the right balance between client needs and agency priorities.

**Interpersonal skills.** You must win the confidence and trust of people before you can persuade them to believe your message. Good interpersonal skills are the key to effective communication. Social scientists have studied and written extensively on how interpersonal relationships are formed and what it takes to develop and maintain them. A study of sociology and psychology will give you an understanding of how trust, interpersonal influence, and mutual expectations can be created.

You must be adaptable so that people with varying levels of ability and intelligence feel comfortable communicating with you. Because you will have to deal with all levels of employees—from clerical staff to line managers to top management—it is important to treat them with equal respect and confidentiality. This can be achieved by emphasizing even little things that affect an individual's self-esteem. You must maintain respect for the dignity of each individual at all times.

The ability to listen without interrupting the speaker is essential to building interpersonal relationships and trust. Good listening demands involvement. A good listener observes the speaker attentively and actively participates in giving feedback. The art of active listening can be acquired with training and practice.

**Empathy.** An understanding of the clients' needs requires sensitivity to the issues, concerns, and people involved. A PR professional must have the ability to listen, and grasp the client's needs quickly.

**Creativity.** Imagination and creativity are the magic ingredients—the product, if you will—that the PR industry "sells." The entire PR package from planning to presentation, calls for creativity.

**Initiative.** PR people must necessarily be self-starters. The ability to identify problems and come up with solutions quickly is an asset.

## EXPERIENCE

Since public relations work covers many kinds of tasks, there is no typical background or "ideal" qualification for public relations professionals. An undergraduate degree is a common entry qualification in the field and is necessary for higher than entry-level jobs. While major study areas may vary, courses or workshops in writing are expected. Most firms require that you have strong writing skills. Many of today's senior PR professionals started in journalism. Public relations practitioners with graduate degrees in communications or business usually command higher salaries than those with only bachelor's degrees.

Some firms do only hire people with specific PR experience. For example, an agency specializing in investor relations may only consider job applicants with experience in that area. Several corporate public affairs departments require at least a minimal experience in a communications job. Senior positions at agencies require several (often four to seven) years of varied public relations experience. Corporations hiring for a management position often look for a PR generalist with an MBA degree, several years of experience, and PRSA accreditation. The Public Relations Society of America has accredited about one third of its members through a standardized examination.

**PRSC accreditation.**   According to the PRSA, an individual of any age who has devoted a substantial portion of time for a period of not less than five years to the paid professional practice of public relations or to the teaching or administration of public relations courses in an accredited college or university and who is currently so engaged may apply for the Accreditation examination. The candidate must first, however, meet the requirements for member status.

Most accreditation candidates find taking the written and oral examination to demonstrate their knowledge and competence in the practice of public relations a rewarding experience. Passing it gives them the right to use "PRSA Accredited" or "APR" in business contacts and also results in an increased sense of professional confidence.

**Internships.**   One of the best ways for students to gain hands-on experience in the field is through an internship program. Educators view internships as a bridge between the fundamentals learned at school and the actual demands of the job environment. Employers view internships as opportunities to develop new talent and a prescreening time for new employees. For the student, the time spent learning while working in a professional environment provides an opportunity to build confidence, earn college credits and often even a stipend, and make contacts.

Many universities have well-established internship programs that provide placement and faculty supervision. The University of Texas-Austin for example, sets up student-run public relations companies. The students go through the process of actually setting up an agency, hiring (choosing) staff, seeking clients, and entering into contracts. Their clients are usually nonprofit organizations.

Some agencies offer student internships each summer for a period of eight to ten weeks and pay a stipend. Large PR firms, like Carl Byoir & Associates, have training programs. One way to learn of internships is to contact the human resource departments at large PR firms and major ad agencies.

## SOURCES OF INFORMATION

**Associations and Societies**

Addresses appear in Appendix B.

The Publicity Club of New York
Public Relations Society of America

## PERIODICALS

*CASE Currents*
*Channels*
*Corporate Communications Report*
*Corporate Shareholder*
*Editor's Newsletter*
*Investor Relations Newsletter*
*IPRA Review*
*Jack O'Dwyer's Newsletter*
*Managing the Human Climate*
*PR Aids' Party Line*
*PR Reporter*
*Public Relations Journal*
*Public Relations News*
*Public Relations Quarterly*
*Public Relations Review*
*Publicist*
*Ragan Report*
*Social Science Monitor*
*Speechwriter's Newsletter*

## DIRECTORIES

*Bacon's International Publicity.* Chicago: Bacon Publishing. Annual.
*Bacon's Publicity Checker: Magazines/Newspaper.* 2 vols. Chicago: Bacon Publishing. Annual.
*Metro California Media.* Washington, DC: Public Relations Plus, Inc. Annual.
*National Trade and Professional Associations.* Washington, DC: Columbia Books. Annual.
*New York Publicity Outlets.* Washington, DC: Public Relations Plus, Inc. Annual.
*O'Dwyer Directory of Corporate Communications.* New York: J.R. O'Dwyer Company. Annual.
*O'Dwyer Directory of Public Relations Firms.* New York: J.R. O'Dwyer Company. Annual.

*Public Relations Journal—Register Issue.* New York: Public Relations Society of America. Annual.

*TV Publicity Outlets Nationwide.* Washington Depot, CT: Public Relations Plus, Inc. Annual.

*TV/Radio Contacts.* New York: Larami Communications. Annual.

*U.S. Publicity Directory.* 5 vols. New York: John Wiley & Sons. Annual.

*Working Press of the Nation.* Burlington, IA: National Research Bureau. Annual.

## RECOMMENDED READING

Bivins, Thomas. *Handbook for Public Relations Writing.* Lincolnwood, IL: NTC Business Books, 1991.

Breen, George and A.B. Blankenship. *Do-It-Yourself Marketing Research.* New York: McGraw-Hill, 1991.

Cutlip and Center. *Effective Public Relations.* 6th ed. Englewood Cliffs, NJ: Prentice-Hall, 1985.

*Dartnell Public Relations Handbook.* 3rd ed. Chicago: Dartnell, 1987.

Goldhaber, G. *Organizational Communication.* Dubuque, IA: W. C. Brown Co., 1979.

Kotler, Philip. *Marketing for Nonprofit Organizations.* Englewood Cliffs, NJ: Prentice-Hall, 1975.

Lesly, Philip. *Lesly's Handbook of Public Relations.* New York: AMACOM, 1991.

Newsom and Scott. *This is PR: Realities of Public Relations.* 4th ed. Belmont, CA: Wadsworth, 1989.

Pesmen, Sandra. *Writing for the Media: Public Relations and the Press.* Lincolnwood, IL: NTC Business Books, 1984.

Reilly, R. *Public Relations in Action.* 2nd ed. Englewood Cliffs, NJ: Prentice-Hall, 1987.

Rotman, Morris B. *Opportunities in Public Relations.* Lincolnwood, IL: VGM Career Horizons, 1988.

Seitel, Fraser. *The Practice of Public Relations.* 4th ed. New York: Macmillan, 1989.

Simon, R. and F. Wylie. *Cases in Public Relations Management.* Lincolnwood, IL: NTC Business Books, 1994.

Saffir, Leonard and John Tanrant. *Power Public Relations.* Lincolnwood, IL: NTC Business Books, 1992.

Yale, David. *The Publicity Handbook.* Lincolnwood, IL: NTC Business Books, 1991.

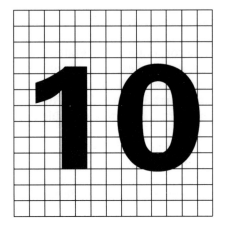

# JOB SEARCH

Communicators have frequently been accused of an inability to communicate. The skill most required in looking for a job is the art of communicating effectively. Expressing yourself clearly in writing and speaking is essential for the two critical steps in landing a job: preparing a résumé and speaking at an interview.

Basic communications skills should be brought into play when looking for a job. You will need to research the job market, write a résumé and cover letters, put together a portfolio, sell your skills (even by using advertising media), and do your own public relations.

While the whole field of communications is growing at a rapid pace, so also is the number of trained people trying to enter the field. The marketplace is truly competitive. Nevertheless, it is possible to get the job you are looking for, if you go about it the right way. Be prepared for hard work and some disappointments too. Looking for a job can, in itself, be a fulltime job.

**Employment Trends**

The traditional job market for professional communicators is changing. While at one time the job market for journalists was limited to national newspapers, the tremendous growth of regional newspapers has expanded the opportunities for today's journalists. In the field of broadcasting, the market was limited to networks and affiliates but has now expanded to independent stations and a growing number of cable channels. In the area of film, while multi-million dollar entertainment productions continue to employ a large number of trained people, the growth of small budget documentaries, and corporate and educational films has expanded the job market.

You must keep track of changing employment trends. New job titles emerge with the birth of new technologies. For example, the title *interactive media designer* came about when more corporations integrated interactive videodiscs into media departments. Another example are jobs for "infotainment" or "infomercial" producers. The need for media people to design and produce programs that can inform as well as "sell" the image or product of a sponsor came about with the growth of cable and low-power television stations.

One way to keep abreast of changing trends in the world of work is by reading trade journals. You should also invest some time in talking to practitioners in fields closely related to your area of work. For example, if you are a corporate video producer, it may prove useful to follow developments in technologies that integrate video and computers.

Your ability to stay on the leading edge of new occupational developments will, in part, depend on your ability to systematically follow national business and economic trends. This can be achieved by reading publications such as *The Wall Street Journal* and the business sections of national newspapers.

## Research

The most critical factor in job hunting is research geared toward targeting a job market. Once you have determined your area of interest and your career goals, you should make a list of potential employers. Each chapter of this book lists the main directory which will provide you with leads to employers in specific fields of communications. Use them to develop your target list. In addition, you should use the membership rosters of associations in the field to identify the names of the hiring executive. Read trade publications that report on people moves within the industry to update your list.

Your research should also include profiles, in particular the need, goals, and philosophy of the organizations where you seek employment. The Dun & Bradstreet directories, Moody's manuals, and Standard & Poor's *Register of Corporations, Directors and Executives* are good sources of information on specific companies. They provide company addresses, telephone numbers, and information on the nature of business, the company's annual sales, and the names of officers and directors. These directories are available in the reference section of public and university libraries.

## Jobs and Career Information Online

If you have access to a computer with a modem, you can obtain career related information through the following channels: commercial online services; electronic bulletin board services; and Internet.

**Commercial online services.** America Online (AOL), CompuServe, and Prodigy are an invaluable source of information on job opportunities. America Online, for example, has a "Career Center" which provides a wide range of job search related information, such as *E-Span* and *Help Wanted-USA* job listings, for basic on-line charges (approximately 10¢ a minute). Numerous special interest groups (SIGs), and electronic forums ranging from Educational T.V., to Broadcasting and Video Production are also accessible through these services; as well as through independent "bulletin boards" and the Internet.

**Bulletin Boards Services (BBSs).** Professional groups, government agencies, special interest groups, and thousands of ordinary folks with a hard disk, a modem, and a dream have established their own BBSs, where information, discussions, and downloadable (retrievable) software are available at little or no cost beyond that of a telephone call.

One example is the State of Virginia Teleconferencing BBS, at modem (804-344-5693 [None,8,1]) or voice (804-344-5590). It offers news about conferences and meetings, teleconferencing and electronic communications, and hundreds of files of related information (including lists of other BBSs).

**Internet.** The Internet is the great "data highway" connecting virtually every university computer and E-Mail system, government agency, major corporation and communication utility in the world.

It is comprised of thousands of separately administered networks, each of these connecting as many as tens of thousands of computers. The total number of individual users of the Internet is in the millions.

Online users might be interested in subscribing to some of the over 3,000 Internet "listservs." Listservs are electronic discussion groups operated on the Internet. They make it possible for participants to discuss topics of professional or personal interest with others who share their interests. For example, the National Association of College Broadcasters (NACB) posts job listings on its *listserv*.

Access to the Internet is available through most institutional and corporate E-Mail systems, Bitnet, commercial services (AOL, CompuServe, Prodigy, etc.), and many other routes. For more information on the Internet, contact your local E-Mail coordinator, computer guru, or *Boardwatch* magazine.

**Contacts**

Many jobs in the communications industry are obtained by word of mouth. That is why it is very important to start making and maintaining contacts with people in your profession at an early stage of your career. You can make contacts with working professionals by joining trade associations. Most national and international trade associations have local chapters that meet frequently. The more you attend these chapter meetings, the greater your opportunity to meet people, as well as learn about new job openings. Another good place to make contacts at are trade fairs, conventions, communications congresses, and conferences. Maintaining contacts is an ongoing process, referred to as *networking*.

Let everyone know the kind of job you are looking for. Creative people often find it difficult to admit that they are looking for a job. But your chances of finding a job will be greater if more people know that you are looking for one. It always helps to meet people who are doing the kind of job you are interested in, to seek their advice on job hunting, as well as for introductions to hiring executives.

**Associations**

A most effective job search method is to work through the various services of professional associations. Many associations offer job placement services, at no cost to the job seeker. For example, the National Association of Educational Broadcasters offers assistance to anyone looking for a position in public broadcasting, through their service called PACT. The NAB operates Employment Clearinghouse (ECH), which is a recorded Jobline featuring current nationwide radio and television station jobs sent to ECH weekly. In addition, association newsletters frequently list job openings.

**Résumé and Cover Letters**

Your résumé must be clear and be designed to meet the job specifications. A résumé is your way of presenting or "selling" your skills to a potential employer. Therefore, it should reflect all pertinent information regarding your education, skills, employment experience, and career goals. A résumé can take many different formats. The format you choose must be one that will set you apart from other applicants, as well as one that will be attractive enough for the hiring executive to grant you an interview. Here are some suggestions in designing your résumé:

- Your résumé should contain your name, address, telephone number, work history, education, awards and honors, professional appointments, associations, and other activities.
- A résumé should not exceed two typewritten pages. Leave enough margin and white space so that it does not look cluttered and is easy to read.
- List your work experience before your education and training. In most production jobs, work experience is valued more than higher education without any experience. All items on your résumé should be listed in reverse chronological order (that is, from present to past).
- Stress the link between your skills and the job responsibilities to be assumed.
- Use action words to indicate your competence.

You will find sample résumés in several books listed in the recommended reading section in each chapter of this book.

Each cover letter should be personalized and targeted to the individual company executive. The cover letter should specify the job or type of work for which you are applying. Keep the cover letter as brief as possible. Remember that the cover letter is your first sales pitch, hence, it should be attention-getting. It should be creative, yet professional. It should be straightforward, lucid, and informative, without repeating the contents of the résumé. Use it as an opportunity to highlight your experience and training that best match the job requirements. End your cover letter with a statement indicating that you will call to set up a personal interview.

**Portfolio**

The main purpose of putting a portfolio together is to display the full range of your skills and abilities. Like a résumé, it should be concise and selective, yet representative of the work you have accomplished. If you are a journalist, your portfolio should not contain clippings of every piece you have written. Select the ones that show a writing style that best suits the readership of the publication at which you seek a job. Photographers should read Chapter 3, which has a section on putting your portfolio together.

Multimedia and video producers could have portfolios that include scripts, photographics, slides, floor plans, and lighting schemes. In the video industry, a good way to demonstrate your skills is with a short videotape of your clips. Your video résumé should showcase excerpts of programs in which you played a key production role. It could also suggest what you are capable of doing as well as provide some insight into your personality. But remember, it must be short: five to six minutes in length is best.

Read the career guidance literature from professional guidance associations that include suggestions on how to put a portfolio together and market your skills. A good portfolio will put you several steps ahead of other job candidates.

**Interview**

The two essential elements to a successful interview are these: be yourself and be prepared. Your dress and manner should be appropriate for the position you are seeking. You should come across as a confident, self-assured person. Be at ease and answer questions in a direct, accurate, and brief manner. Don't try to please. Use your responses to emphasize your strengths.

Being prepared involves thoroughly researching the organization. Find out a little bit about the person you are interviewing with if you can. This will help you establish any grounds of common interests that will set the tone for a warm and productive interview. Also find out as much as possible about the company and its clients. Discuss the company's needs and your abilities to help meet them. This should impress the interviewer. It will demonstrate your interest in and enthusiasm for the organization and will establish an image of you as a bright and intelligent person.

You may ask questions as the interview progresses. It is customary, however, to wait until asked if you have any questions. Be careful not to control the interviewer or to talk too much; interviews should be interactive.

Follow up your interview with a letter of thanks. It should be brief and include a sentence reinforcing your interest in the job.

## RECOMMENDED READING

A job search can be very demanding. There are many books that can guide you in your endeavors to find a position that will best suit your abilities. Here are some suggestions.

Bloch, Deborah Perlmutter. *How to Write a Winning Résumé.* Lincolnwood, IL: VGM Career Horizons, 1994.

Bolles, Richard. *What Color Is Your Parachute?* Berkeley, CA: Ten Speed Press. Updated annually.

Kennedy, Joyce Lain and Daryll Laramore, *Joyce Lain Kennedy's Career Book.* 2nd ed. Lincolnwood, IL: VGM Career Horizons, 1992.

Langhome, Karyn E. and Eric R. Martin. *Cover Letters They Don't Forget.* Lincolnwood, IL: VGM Career Horizons, 1993.

Lott, Catherine S., and Lott, Oscar C. *How To Land a Better Job.* Lincolnwood, IL: VGM Career Horizons, 1989.

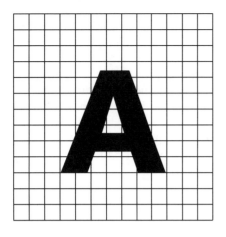

# ASSOCIATIONS AND SOCIETIES

The Academy of Motion Picture Arts &
  Sciences
8949 Wilshire Blvd.
Beverly Hills, CA 90211

Acoustical Society of America
500 Sunnyside Blvd.
Woodbury, NY 11797

Actors' Equity Association
165 W. 46th St.
New York, NY 10036

The Advertising Club of New York
155 E. 55th St., Suite 202
New York, NY 10022

The Advertising Council
825 Third Ave.
New York, NY 10022

Advertising Photographers of America, Inc.
  (APA)
27 West 20th Street
New York, NY 10011

Advertising Research Foundation
3 East 54th St.
New York, NY 10022

Advertising Women of New York
153 E. 57th St.
New York, NY 10022

Alliance of Motion Picture and Television
  Producers
14144 Ventura Blvd., 3rd fl.
Sherman Oaks, CA 91423

American Advertising Federation
1400 K. St. N.W., Suite 1000
Washington, DC 20005

American Association of Advertising
  Agencies
666 3rd Ave.
New York, NY 10017

American Cinema Editors
2410 Beverly Blvd., Suite 1
Los Angeles, CA 90057

American Institute of Graphic Arts
1059 Third Ave.
New York, NY 10021

American Marketing Association
250 S. Wacker Dr., Suite 200
Chicago, IL 60600

American Newspaper Publishers
  Association
The Newspaper Center
P.O. Box 17407, Dulles International
  Airport
Washington, DC 20041

American Society for Training &
  Development (ASTD)
Box 1443
1630 Duke Street
Alexandria, VA 22313

American Society of Cinematographers,
  Inc.
1782 North Orange Drive
Hollywood, CA 90028

American Society of Magazine Editors
575 Lexington Ave.
New York, NY 10022

American Society of Magazine
  Photographers (ASMP)
419 Park Avenue, Suite 1407
New York, NY 10016

American Society of Newspaper Editors
Box 17004, Washington, DC 20041

American Society of Picture Professionals
  (ASPP)
Box 5283, Grand Central Station
New York, NY 10163

American Society of Photogrammetry
  (ASP) and Remote Sensing
5410 Grosvenor Lane, Suite 210
Bethesda, MD 20814-2160

American Video Association
2885 N. Nevada St., #140
Chandler, AZ 85225

American Women in Radio and Television
1101 Connecticut Ave, N.W., Suite 700
Washington, DC 20036

Arts Directors Club of New York
250 Park Ave. S.
New York, NY 10003

Associated Press Broadcasters Association
1825 K St. N.W., Suite 615
Washington, DC 20006

Association for Multi-Image International,
  Inc. (AMI)
8019 N. Himes Avenue, Suite 401
Tampa, FL 33614

Association for Educational
  Communications & Technologies (AECT)
1126 Sixteenth Street, N.W., Suite 310
Washington, DC 20036

Association of Audio-Visual Technicians
  (AAVT)
P.O. Box 9716
2378 S. Broadway
Denver, CO 80210

Association of Independent TV Stations
(INTV)
1200 18th Street, N.W., Suite 508
Washington, DC 20036

Association of Independent Video &
Filmmakers (AIVF)
625 Broadway, 9th Floor
New York, NY 10012

Association of National Advertisers
155 E. 44th St.
New York, NY 10017

Association of Professional Color
Laboratories (APCL)
3000 Picture Pl.
Jackson, MI 49201

Association of Visual Communicators
(formerly Information Film Producers of
America, (IFPA))
31942 Kingspark Ct.
Westlake Village, CA 91631

Audio Engineering Society (AES)
60 East 42nd Street, Rm. 2520
New York, NY 10065

Audio Visual Management Association
(AVMA)
Box 656 Downtown Station
7907 N.W. 53rd St., Suite 346
Miami, FL 33166

Biological Photographers Association (BPA)
115 Stoneridge Dr.
Chapel Hill, NC 27514

Broadcast Education Association
1771 N Street, N.W.
Washington, DC 20036

Business/Professional Advertising
Association
901 N. Washington St., Suite 206
Alexandria, VA 22314

Cable Television Advertising Bureau, Inc.
757 Third Avenue
New York, NY 10017

Cable Television Administration &
  Marketing Society
635 Slaters Lane, Suite 250
Alexandria, VA 23314

Cable Television Advertising Bureau
757 Third Avenue
New York, NY 10017

Cable Television Information Center
P.O. Box 1205
Annandale, VA 22003

Chicago Women in Publishing (CWIP)
645 N. Michigan Ave., Suite 1058
Chicago, IL 60611

Council of Sales Promotion Agencies
750 Summer St.
Stamford, CT 06901

Direct Marketing Association
11 W. 42nd St.
New York, NY 10036-8096

Directors Guild of America (Film)
7920 Sunset Boulevard
Hollywood, CA 90046

Evidence Photographers International
  Council (EPIC)
600 Main St.
Honesdale, PA 18431

Feminist Writers Guild
P.O. Box 14055
Chicago, IL 60614

Institute for Public Relations Research and
  Education
310 Madison Ave., Suite 1710
New York, NY 10017

Health Education Media Association
  (HEMA)
P.O. Box 771
Riverdale, GA 30274

Health Sciences Communications
  Association (HeSCA)
6105 Lindell Blvd.
St. Louis, MO 63112

Institute of Outdoor Advertising
342 Madison Avenue
New York, NY 10173

InterAmerican Press Association
2911 N.W., 39th Street
Miami, FL 33142

International Association of Business
Communicators (IABC)
One Hallidie Plaza, Suite 600
San Francisco, CA 94102

International Association of Satellite Users
and Suppliers
P.O. Box DD
McLean, VA 22101

International Circulation Managers
Association
Box 17420, Dulles Airport
Washington, DC 20041

International Communications Industries
Association (ICIA)
3150 Spring Street
Fairfax, VA 22031

International Radio & Television Society
420 Lexington Avenue
New York, NY 10170

International Tape/Disc Association (ITA)
505 Eighth Ave.
New York, NY 10018

International Teleconferencing Association
(ITCA)
1150 Connecticut Avenue N.W., Suite 1050
Washington, DC 20036

International Television Association (ITVA)
6311 N. O'Connor, LB51
Irving, TX 75039

Institute of Electrical & Electronics
Engineers (IEEE)
345 East 47th Street
New York, NY 10017

Investigative Reporters and Editors, Inc.
100 Neff Hall
Univ. of Missouri
Columbia, MO 65211

Magazine Publishers Association
575 Lexington Ave.
New York, NY 10022

National Academy of Recording Arts &
    Sciences (NARAS)
303 N. Glenoaks Blvd., Suite 140 mez
Burbank, CA 91502-1178

National Academy of Television Arts and
    Sciences
New York Chapter
1560 Broadway, Suite 503
New York, NY 10036

National Advertising Review Board
845 Third Ave.
New York, NY 10022

National Alliance for Women in
    Communications Industries
P.O. Box 33984
Washington, DC 20033

National Association of Black Owned
    Broadcasters
1730 M Street, N.W., Room 412
Washington, DC 20036

National Association of Broadcast
    Employees & Technicians
(NABET 700)
7101 Wisconsin Ave., Suite 800
Bethesda, MD 20814

National Association of Broadcasters (NAB)
1771 N Street, N.W.
Washington, DC 20036

National Association of Publisher
    Representatives
295 5th Ave., Suite 621
New York, NY 10016

National Association of Recording
  Merchandisers (NARM)
3 Eves Dr., Suite 307
Marlton, NJ 08053

National Association of Science Writers
P.O. Box 294
Greenlawn, NY 11740

National Association of Television Program
  Executives (NATPE)
10100 Santa Monica Blvd., Suite 300
Los Angeles, CA 90067

National Cable Television Association
  (NCTA)
1724 Massachusetts Avenue, N.W.
Washington, DC 20036

National Computer Graphics Association
  (NCGA)
2722 Merrilee Drive, Suite 200
Fairfax, VA 22031

National Conference of Editorial Writers
6223 Executive Blvd.
Rockville, MD 20852

National Federation of Local Cable
  Programmers
P.O. Box 27290
Washington, DC 20038

National Institute for Low Power Television
c/o Global Village
431 Broome St.
New York, NY 10013

National Newspaper Association
1627 K St., N.W., Suite 400
Washington, DC 20006

National Press Photographers Association
  (NPPA)
3200 Crousdale Dr., Suite 306
Durham, NC 27705

National Religious Broadcasters Association
  (NRBA)
P.O. Box 1926
Morristown, NJ 07960

Newspaper Advertising Bureau, Inc.
1180 Avenue of the Americas
New York, NY 10036

The Newspaper Guild
8611 Second Ave.
Silver Springs, MD 20910

Point of Purchase Advertising Institute
66 N. Van Brunt St.
Englewood, NJ 07631

Premium Advertising Association of
  America
322 Eighth Ave., Suite 1201
New York, NY 10001

Print Advertising Association
10-64 Jackson Ave.
Long Island City, NY 11101

Producers Guild of America
400 S. Beverly Dr., Rm 211
Beverly Hills, CA 90212

Professional Photographers of America
(PP of A)
1090 Executive Way
Des Plaines, IL 60018

Promotional Marketing Association of
  America
322 Eighth Avenue, Suite 1201
New York, NY 10001

Public Service Satellite Consortium (PSSC)
88 St. Stephen Street
Boston, MA 02115

Public Relations Society of America
33 Irving Pl., 3rd Fl.
New York, NY 10003

Radio Advertising Bureau
304 Park Ave. S.
New York, NY 10010

Radio-Television News Directors Association
1717 K St. N.W., Suite 615
Washington, DC 20006

Recording Industry Association of America,
    Inc. (RIAA)
1020 19th St. N.W., Suite 200
Washington, DC 20036

Screen Actors Guild
7065 Hollywood Blvd.
Hollywood, CA 90028

Society for Photographic Education (SPE)
Campus Box 318, Univ. of Colorado
Boulder, CO 80309

Society of Broadcast Engineers
P.O. Box 20450
Indianapolis, IN 46220

Society of Cable Television Engineers
    (SCTE)
669 Exton Commons
Exton, PA 19341

Society of Illustrators
128 East 63rd Street
New York, NY 10021

Society of Motion Picture & Television
    Engineers (SMPTE)
595 W. Hartsdale Ave.
White Plains, NY 10607

Society of National Association
    Publications
3299 K St. N.W., 7th Fl.
Washington, DC 20007

Society of Photo-Technologists (SPT)
P.O. Box 9634
6535 S. Dayton, Suite 2000
Englewood, CO 80111

Society of Professional Audio Recording
    Studios (SPARS)
4300 Tenth Ave. N.
Lake Worth, FL 33461

Society of Professional Journalists
(Sigma Delta Chi)
c/o 53 W. Jackson Blvd., Suite 731
Chicago, IL 60604

Specialty Advertising Association
  International
1404 Walnut Hill Lane
Irving, TX 75038-3094

Suburban Newspapers of America
111 E. Wacker Drive
Chicago, IL 60611

Television Bureau of Advertising
477 Madison Ave.
New York, NY 10022

Videotex Industry Association
8403 Colesville Rd., Suite 865
Silver Spring, MD 20910-3366

Wedding Photographers International
  (WPI)
P.O. Box 2003
1312 Lincoln Blvd.
Santa Monica, CA 90406

Women in Communications
2101 Wilson Blvd., Suite 417
Arlington, VA 22201

Women in Cable
500 N. Michigan Ave., Suite 1400
Chicago, IL 60611

Women in Film
6464 Sunset Blvd., Suite 660
Hollywood, CA 90028

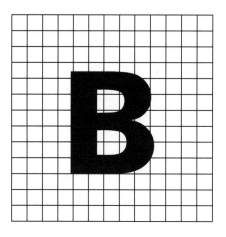

*Ad East*
AdEast Enterprises, Inc.
907 Park Square Blvd.
Boston, MA 02116

*Ad Forum*
Agency File, Inc.
820 Second Avenue
New York, NY 10017

*Advanced Imaging*
50 W. 23rd St.
New York, NY 10010

*Advertising Age*
Crain Communications, Inc.
740 N. Rush Street
Chicago, IL 60611

*Advertising and Communications Yellow
  Pages*
New York Yellow Pages, Inc.
113 University Place
New York, NY 10003

*Advertising/Communications Times*
121 Chestnut Street
Philadelphia, PA 19106

*Advertising World*
Directories International, Inc.
150 Fifth Avenue
New York, NY 10011

*Adweek*
ASM Communications, Inc.
820 Second Avenue
New York, NY 10017

*AES Journal* (Audio Engineering Society)
60 East 42nd Street
New York, NY 10165

*Amazing Cinema*
12 Moray Court
Baltimore, MD 21236

*American Film*
American Film Institute
J.F.K. Center
Washington, DC 20566

*American Cinematographer*
1782 N. Orange Drive
Hollywood, CA 90028

*American Newspaper Markets Circulation*
P.O. Box 994
2701 Barrymore
Malibu, CA 90265

*American Photographer*
1515 Broadway
New York, NY 10036

*Aperture*
20 E. 23rd St.
New York, NY 10010

*Art Direction*
10 East 39th Street
New York, NY 10016

*Art Product News*
In-Art Publishing Company
P.O. Drawer 117
St. Petersburg, FL 33731

*AV Video*
Montage Publishing, Inc.
701 Westchester Avenue
White Plains, NY 10604

*Bacon's International Publicity Checker*
Bacon Publishing Co.
14 E. Jackson
Chicago, IL 60604

*Backstage/Backstage Shoot*
BPI Publishing
1515 Broadway
New York, NY 10036

*The Big Reel*
Box 239 A
Madison, NC 27025

*Boxoffice*
623 South Wabash Avenue, Suite 316
Hollywood, CA 90028

*Briefings*
Advertising Specialty Institute
Bucks County Business Park
1120 Wheelerway
Langhorne, PA 19047

*Broadcast Engineering (BE)*
Intertec Publishing Corporation
9800 Metcalf
Overland Park, KS 66212

*Broadcasting & Cable*
P.O. Box 6399
Torrance, CA 90504

*Business Marketing*
Crain Communications, Inc.
740 North Rush Street
Chicago, IL 60611

*Cable Age*
1270 Avenue of the Americas
New York, NY 10020

*Cable Marketing*
352 Park Ave. South
New York, NY 10016

*Cable News*
7315 Wisconsin Ave., Suite 1200N
Bethesda, MD 20814

*Cablevision*
P.O. Box 5400 T.A.
Denver, CO 60217

*CASE Currents*
CASE
One Dupont Circle
Washington, DC 20036

*CAT Journal*
4209 NW 23rd, Suite 109
Oklahoma City, OK 73101

*CD-ROM Professional*
Pemberton Press Inc.
462 Danbury Road
Wilton, CT 06897

*CD-ROM World*
Meckler Corporation
11 Ferry Lane West
Westport, CT 06880

*Channels*
Public Relations Society of America
1515 Broadway
New York, NY 10036

*Cineaste*
200 Park Ave. South
New York, NY 10003

*Cinefantastique*
P.O. Box 270
Oak Park, IL 60303

*Cinemagic*
475 Park Ave. South
New York, NY 10016

*Columbia Journalism Review*
Graduate School of Journalism
Columbia University
New York, NY 10027

*Communication Arts*
Coyne & Blanchard
P.O. Box 10300
400 Sherman
Palo Alto, CA 94303

*Computer Pictures*
701 Westchester Avenue
White Plains, NY 10604

*Consumer Electronics*
1836 Jefferson Pl., N.W.
Washington, DC 10036

*Corporate Shareholder*
271 Madison Ave.
New York, NY 10016

*Creative*
Magazines/Creative, Inc.
37 West 39th St.
New York, NY 10018

*The Creative Black Book* (also *The Black
    Book)*
Friendly Press, Inc.
401 Park Ave. South
New York, NY 10016

*Darkroom & Creative Camera Techniques*
P.O. Box 48312
Niles, IL 60648

*Darkroom Photography*
One Hallide Plaza
San Francisco, CA 94102

*Dartnell Sales and Marketing Service
    Executive Report*
Dartnell Corp.
4660 North Ravenswood
Chicago, IL 60640

*dB, The Sound Engineering Magazine*
Sagamore Publishing Co., Inc.
1120 Old Country Rd.
Plainview, NY 11803

*Desktop Video World*
TechMedia Publishing Inc./IDG Co.
80 Elm Street
Peterborough, NH 03458

*Direct Marketing*
Hoke Communications, Inc.
224 Seventh St.
Garden City, NY 11530

*The Direct Marketing Market Place*
Hilary House Publishers, Inc.
1033 Channel Drive
Hewlett, NY 11557

*Directory of Educational Programs*
Audio Engineering Society
60 E. 42nd St.
New York, NY 10165

*DM News: The Newspaper of Direct Marketing*
Mill Hollow Corp.
19 West 21st St.
New York, NY 10010

*Editor and Publisher*
575 Lexington Ave.
New York, NY 10022

*Editor's Newsletter*
P.O. Box 243
Lenox Hill Station
New York, NY 10021

*Fast Forward*
Association of Audiovisual Technicians
P.O. Box 9716
Denver, CO 80209

*Film & Video*
Optic Music, Inc.
8455 Beverly Blvd., Suite 508
Los Angeles, CA 90048

*Film Comment*
Film Society of Lincoln Center
140 W. 65th St.
New York, NY 10023

*The Film Journal*
1600 Broadway
New York, NY 10019

*Films in Review*
P.O. Box 589
New York, NY 10021

*Film Quarterly*
University of California Press
Berkeley, CA 94720

*Film News*
250 West 57th Street, Room 1527
New York, NY 10019

*The Folio: The Magazine of Magazine
 Management*
Folio Publishing Corp.
P.O. Box 697
125 Elm Street
New Canaan, CT 06840

*FYI, For Your Information*
448 Raintree Ct.
Glen Ellyn, IL 60137

*The Gallagher Report*
230 Park Ave.
New York, NY 10017

*Graphic Design: USA*
Kaye Publishing Corp.
120 E. 56th St.
New York, NY 10022

*The Hollywood Reporter*
P.O. Box 1431
Hollywood, CA 90028

*The Hollywood Studio Magazine*
P.O. Box 1566
Apple Valley, CA 92307

*Hope Reports, Inc.*
58 Carverdale Drive
Rochester, NY 14618

*The Illustrated Audio Equipment Reference
 Catalog*
Bill Daniels Co.
Shawnee, KS

*Imaging Magazine*
Telecom Library Inc.
12 West 21st Street
New York, NY 10010

*The Independent*
625 Broadway, 9th Floor
New York, NY 10012

*Index/Directory of Women's Media*
Women's Institute for Freedom of the Press
3306 Ross Place, N.W.
Washington, DC 20008

*Industrial Photography*
PTN Publishing Company
445 Broad Hollow Road
Melville, NY 11747

*International Advertiser*
Roth International
615 West 22nd Street
Oak Brook, IL 60521

*International Musician and Recording World*
Gulf & Western Bldg.
15 Columbus Circle
New York, NY 10023

*International Recording Equipment and
    Studio Directory*
Billboard Publications, Inc.
1515 Broadway
New York, NY 10036

*Investor Relations Newsletter*
Enterprise Publications
20 N. Wacker Dr.
Chicago, IL 60606

*IPRA Review*
50 Pine Grove
London N20 8LA

*Journal of Advertising Research*
The Advertising Research Foundation
3 E. 54th St.
New York, NY 10022

*Journal of Communication*
Annenberg School Press
P.O. Box 13358
Philadelphia, PA 19101

*Journal of Marketing*
*Journal of Marketing Research*
The American Marketing Association
250 S. Wacker Drive
Chicago, IL 60606

*Journal of the University Film and Video*
  *Association*
Southern Illinois University
Carbondale, IL 62901

*Journalism History*
California State University at Northridge
Northridge, CA 91330

*Journalism Quarterly*
School of Journalism
Ohio University
Athens, OH 45701

*Lens' On Campus*
645 Stewart Ave.
Garden City, NY 11530

*Literature/Film Quarterly*
Salisbury State College
Salisbury, MD 28101

*Madison Avenue*
Madison Avenue Publishing Corp.
369 Lexington Avenue
New York, NY 10017

*Magazine Age*
Freed Crown Lee Publishing, Inc.
225 Park Avenue
New York, NY 10169

*Magazine and Bookseller*
North American Publishing Co.
545 Madison Ave.
New York, NY 10022

*Managing the Human Climate*
Lesly Co.
130 E. Randolph
Chicago, IL 60601

*Marketing and Media Decisions*
Decisions Publications, Inc.
1140 Avenue of the Americas
New York, NY 10036

*The Masthead*
National Conference of Editorial Writers
6223 Executive Blvd.
Rockville, MD 20852

*Metro California Media*
P.O. Box 327
Washington Depot, CT 06794

*Midwest Media Directory*
176 W. Adams
Chicago, IL 60690

*Millimeter*
826 Broadway
New York, NY 10003

*Mix*
2608 Ninth Street
Berkeley, CA 94710

*Movie Trends*
P.O. Box 173
Glen Clove, NY 11542

*Multi-Images Journal* (AMI)
8019 N. Himes Ave., Suite 401
Tampa, FL 33614

*National Trade/Professional Associations*
Columbia Books
734 15th St. N.W.
Washington, DC 20005

*New Media*
Hypermedia Communications Inc.
901 Mariner's Island Blvd., Suite 365
San Mateo, CA 94404

*New York Production Guide*
150 Fifth Ave., Suite 219
New York, NY 10011

*New York Publicity Outlets*
P.O. Box 327
Washington Depot, CT 06794

*News Photographer*
School of Journalism
Bowling Green State University
Bowling Green, OH 43043

*O'Dwyer Directory of Public Relations*
  *Executives*
*O'Dwyer Directory of Public Relations*
  *Firms*
*O'Dwyer's Directory of Corporate*
  *Communications*
*O'Dwyer's Newsletter*
271 Madison Ave.
New York, NY 10016

*On Location*
6777 Hollywood Blvd., Suite 501
Hollywood, CA 90028

*Personal Publishing*
The Renegade Company
P.O. Box 390
Itasca, IL 60143

*Petersen's PhotoGraphic*
8490 Sunset Blvd.
Los Angeles, CA 90028

*Photo/Design*
1515 Broadway
New York, NY 10036

*Photo District News*
49 E. 21st St.
New York, NY 10010

*Photo/Electronic Imaging*
1312 Lincoln Blvd.
Santa Monica, CA 90406

*Photo Marketing*
3000 Picture Pl.
Jackson, MI 49201

*Photo Weekly*
1515 Broadway
New York, NY 10036

*Photogrammetric Engineering and Remote
    Sensing*
210 Little Falls St.
Falls Church, VA 22046

*Photographer's Market*
Writer's Digest Books
9933 Alliance Rd.
Cincinnati, OH 45242

*Photographic Science and Engineering*
7003 Kilworth Lane
Springfield, VA 22151

*Photographic Trade News*
101 Crossways Park West
Woodbury, NY 11797

*Popular Photography*
1633 Broadway
New York, NY 10019

*Potentials in Marketing*
50 S. 9th St.
Minneapolis, MN 55402

*PR Aids' Party Line*
221 Park Ave. South
New York, NY 10003

*PR Reporter*
P.O. Box 600
Exeter, NH 03833

*Print*
355 Lexington Avenue
New York, NY 10017

*The Producer's Masterguide*
330 West 42nd Street, 16th Floor
New York, New York 10036

*Pro Sound News*
2 Park Avenue
New York, NY 10016

*The Professional Photographer*
1090 Executive Way
Des Plaines, IL 60018

*Public Opinion Quarterly*
American Association of Public Opinion
   and Research
7000 Journalism Bldg.
Graduate School of Journalism
Columbia University
New York, NY 10027

*Public Relations Journal*
*Public Relations Register*
Public Relations Society of America
1515 Broadway
New York, NY 10036

*Public Relations News*
127 E. 80th St.
New York, NY 10021

*Public Relations Quarterly*
44 W. Market St.
Rhinebeck, NY 12572

*Public Relations Review*
7338 Baltimore Blvd. #101A
College Park, MD 20740

*Publicist*
221 Park Ave. South
New York, NY 10003

*Publishers Weekly*
R. R. Bowker Company
205 E. 42nd St.
New York, NY 10017

*Quarterly Review of Film Studies*
P.O. Box 67
South Salem, NY 10590

*Quill*
Society of Professional Journalists
840 North Lake Shore Drive, Suite 801
Chicago, IL 60611

*Radio & Records*
1930 Century Park West
Los Angeles, CA 90067

*Radio World*
5827 Columbia Pike, Ste. 310
Falls Church, VA 22041

*Ragan Report*
Ragan Communications
407 S. Dearborn
Chicago, IL 60605

*The Rangefinder*
1312 Lincoln Blvd.
Santa Monica, CA 90406

*Religious Broadcasting*
NRBA, CN 1926
Morristown, NJ 07960

*S & VC (Sound & Video Contractor)*
9800 Metcalf
Overland Park, KS 66215

*Signs of the Times*
407 Gilbert Avenue
Cincinnati, OH 45202

*Small Press*
Meckler Publishing Corp.
11 Ferry Lane West
Westport, CT 06880

*Social Science Monitor*
7338 Baltimore Blvd. #101A
College Park, MD 20740

*Sound Management*
Radio Advertising Bureau
485 Lexington Avenue
New York, NY 10017

*Specialty Advertising Business*
1404 Walnut Hill Lane
Irving, TX 75062

*Speechwriter's Newsletter*
Ragan Communications
407 S. Dearborn
Chicago, IL 60605

*Standard Directory of Advertisers*
*Standard Directory of Advertising Agencies*
  *(Agency Red Book)*
*Standard Rate & Data Service*
3005 Glenview Road
Wilmette, IL 60091

*Studio Photography*
101 Crossways Park West
Woodbury, NY 11797

*Teleconference*
Applied Business Telecommunication
2401 Crow Canyon Road, Suite 310
San Ramon, CA 94583

*Telespan Newsletter*
50 W. Palm St.
Altadena, CA 91001

*Television Digest*
Warren Publishing Inc.
475 Fifth Avenue
New York, NY 10017

*Television Radio Age*
1270 Avenue of the Americas
New York, NY 10020

*T.H.E Journal*
Technological Horizons in Education
150 El Camino Real, Suite 112
Tustin, CA 92680

*Training*
50 S. 9th St.
Minneapolis, MN 55402

*TV Digest*
1836 Jefferson Pl., N.W.
Washington, DC 10036

*TV Publicity Outlets Nationwide*
P.O. Box 327
Washington Depot, CT 06794

*TV/Radio Contacts*
Larami Inc.
151 E. 50th St.
New York, NY 10022

*TV Technology*
Industrial Marketing Advisory Services Inc.
5827 Columbia Pike, Suite 310
Falls Church, VA 22041

*U.S. Publicity Directory*
John Wiley & Sons
605 Third Ave.
New York, NY 10158

*Variety*
154 W. 46th St.
New York, NY 10036

*Video Systems*
Intertec Publishing Corporation
9800 Metcalf
Overland Park, KS 66212

*Videography*
PSN Publications
2 Park Avenue, Suite 1820
New York, NY 10016

*(The) Video Register*
Knowledge Industry Publications Inc.
701 Westchester Avenue
White Plains, NY 10604

*Video Systems*
Intertec Publishing Corp.
9800 Metcalf
Overland Park, KS 66212

*Video Technology News*
Phillips Publishing Co.
7811 Montrose Road
Potomac, MD 20854

*Washington Journalism Review*
233 Wisconsin Ave.
Washington, DC 20007

*Working Press of the Nation*
National Research Bureau
Burlington, IA 52601

*Writer's Market*
Writer's Digest Books
9933 Alliance Road
Cincinnati, Ohio 45242

*Zip/Target Marketing*
401 North Broad Street
Philadelphia, PA 19108

# VGM CAREER BOOKS/CAREERS FOR YOU

## OPPORTUNITIES IN

Accounting
Acting
Advertising
Aerospace
Agriculture
Airline
Animal and Pet Care
Architecture
Automotive Service
Banking
Beauty Culture
Biological Sciences
Biotechnology
Book Publishing
Broadcasting
Building Construction Trades
Business Communication
Business Management
Cable Television
CAD/CAM
Carpentry
Chemistry
Child Care
Chiropractic
Civil Engineering
Cleaning Service
Commercial Art and Graphic Design
Computer Maintenance
Computer Science
Counseling & Development
Crafts
Culinary
Customer Service
Data Processing
Dental Care
Desktop Publishing
Direct Marketing
Drafting
Electrical Trades
Electronic and Electrical Engineering
Electronics
Energy
Engineering
Engineering Technology
Environmental
Eye Care
Fashion
Fast Food
Federal Government
Film
Financial
Fire Protection Services
Fitness
Food Services
Foreign Language
Forestry
Government Service
Health and Medical
High Tech
Home Economics
Homecare Services
Hospital Administration
Hotel & Motel Management
Human Resources Management
   Careers
Information Systems
Insurance
Interior Design
International Business
Journalism
Laser Technology
Law
Law Enforcement and Criminal
   Justice
Library and Information Science
Machine Trades
Magazine Publishing

Marine & Maritime
Masonry
Marketing
Materials Science
Mechanical Engineering
Medical Imaging
Medical Technology
Metalworking
Microelectronics
Military
Modeling
Music
Newspaper Publishing
Nonprofit Organizations
Nursing
Nutrition
Occupational Therapy
Office Occupations
Packaging Science
Paralegal Careers
Paramedical Careers
Part-time & Summer Jobs
Performing Arts
Petroleum
Pharmacy
Photography
Physical Therapy
Physician
Plastics
Plumbing & Pipe Fitting
Postal Service
Printing
Property Management
Psychology
Public Health
Public Relations
Purchasing
Real Estate
Recreation and Leisure
Refrigeration and Air Conditioning
Religious Service
Restaurant
Retailing
Robotics
Sales
Secretarial
Securities
Social Science
Social Work
Speech-Language Pathology
Sports & Athletics
Sports Medicine
State and Local Government
Teaching
Technical Communications
Telecommunications
Television and Video
Theatrical Design & Production
Tool and Die
Transportation
Travel
Trucking
Veterinary Medicine
Visual Arts
Vocational and Technical
Warehousing
Waste Management
Welding
Word Processing
Writing
Your Own Service Business

**CAREERS IN** Accounting; Advertising;
Business; Communications; Computers;
Education; Engineering; Finance;
Health Care; High Tech; Law;
Marketing; Medicine; Science; Social
and Rehabilitation Services

## CAREER DIRECTORIES

Careers Encyclopedia
Dictionary of Occupational Titles
Occupational Outlook Handbook

## CAREER PLANNING

Admissions Guide to Selective
   Business Schools
Beginning Entrepreneur
Career Planning and Development
   for College Students and Recent
   Graduates
Careers Checklists
Careers for Animal Lovers
Careers for Bookworms
Careers for Computer Buffs
Careers for Crafty People
Careers for Culture Lovers
Careers for Environmental Types
Careers for Film Buffs
Careers for Foreign Language
   Aficionados
Careers for Good Samaritans
Careers for Gourmets
Careers for Nature Lovers
Careers for Numbers Crunchers
Careers for Sport Nuts
Careers for Travel Buffs
Cover Letters They Don't Forget
Guide to Basic Resume Writing
How to Approach an Advertising Agency
   and Walk Away with the Job You Want
How to Bounce Back Quickly After
   Losing Your Job
How to Change Your Career
How to Choose the Right Career
How to Get and Keep
   Your First Job
How to Get into the Right Law School
How to Get People to Do Things
   Your Way
How to Have a Winning Job Interview
How to Jump Start a Stalled Career
How to Land a Better Job
How to Launch Your Career in
   TV News
How to Make the Right Career Moves
How to Market Your College Degree
How to Move from College into a
   Secure Job
How to Negotiate the Raise
   You Deserve
How to Prepare a *Curriculum Vitae*
How to Prepare for College
How to Run Your Own Home Business
How to Succeed in College
How to Succeed in High School
How to Write a Winning Resume
How to Write Your College
   Application Essay
Joyce Lain Kennedy's Career Book
Resumes for Advertising Careers
Resumes for Banking and Financial
   Careers
Resumes for College Students &
   Recent Graduates
Resumes for Communications Careers
Resumes for Education Careers
Resumes for Health and Medical Careers
Resumes for High School Graduates
Resumes for High Tech Careers
Resumes for Midcareer Job Changes
Resumes for Sales and Marketing Careers
Resumes for Scientific and Technical
   Careers
Successful Interviewing for College
   Seniors

**VGM Career Horizons**
a division of *NTC Publishing Group*
4255 West Touhy Avenue
Lincolnwood, Illinois 60646-1975